# THE APOSTLES' CREED

# THE
# APOSTLES' CREED

*Its Origin, Its Purpose, and
Its Historical Interpretation*

A Lecture, with Critical Notes

BY

ARTHUR CUSHMAN McGIFFERT

Washburn Professor of Church History in the Union Theological
Seminary, New York

*Wipf and Stock Publishers*
150 West Broadway • Eugene OR 97401
2001

The Apostle's Creed
*Its Origin, Its Purpose, and Its Historcal*
By McGiffert, Arthur Cushman
ISBN: 1-57910-665-x

Reprinted by *Wipf and Stock Publishers*
150 West Broadway • Eugene OR 97401

Previously published by T & T Clark, Edinburgh, 1902.

# PREFACE

THE lecture with which this volume opens was first given at the Harvard University Summer School of Theology in July, 1899. It has been given since at the University of Chicago, and a part of it was read at the meeting of the American Historical Association held in Detroit in December, 1900. The lecture is printed substantially in its original form, though at a few points changes have been made as a result of further study. Its publication has been deferred until the present time because it contains some conclusions at variance with those commonly accepted by modern scholars, which it seemed best to withhold until the reasons for them could be stated in detail. Those reasons will be found in the critical notes, which fill the greater part of the volume, and contain discussions of the most important questions connected with the origin, the text, the purpose and historical interpretation of the creed. Since the appearance last year of the final volume of Kattenbusch's elaborate monograph on the Apostles' Creed I have worked over the whole subject again and have tested my conclusions in its light. As I am compelled to disagree with Kattenbusch at many points I wish to bear testimony here to the value of his work, which is the most exhaustive treatment of the subject we have and, in spite of some serious defects in method, will be indispensable to all future workers in this particular field.

It will be seen that the notes deal largely with the Old Roman Symbol and not with the present text of the creed. This is due not only to the greater relative importance of the former, but also to the fact that my own independent investigations have been confined to questions connected with the older symbol, and I have not cared to burden the notes with second-hand results. The conclusions touching the origin and history of the present text of the creed which are given in the latter part of the lecture are based wholly upon the investigations of others, especially Caspari and Kattenbusch.

To my colleague, Prof. James Everett Frame, my hearty thanks are due for the valuable assistance he has rendered me in connection with the revision of the proof sheets.

# CONTENTS

LECTURE . . . . . . . . . . . . . 3

CRITICAL NOTES:

    I. THE TEXT OF THE OLD ROMAN SYMBOL IN THE FOURTH CENTURY . . . . . . . 39

    II. THE DATE OF THE OLD ROMAN SYMBOL . . 46

    III. THE ORIGINAL TEXT OF THE OLD ROMAN SYMBOL . . . . . . . . . . . 84

    IV. THE PLACE OF COMPOSITION OF THE OLD ROMAN SYMBOL . . . . . . . . . 101

    V. THE PURPOSE OF THE OLD ROMAN SYMBOL AND ITS HISTORICAL INTERPRETATION . . 105

    VI. THE OLD ROMAN SYMBOL AND THE BAPTISMAL FORMULA . . . . . . . . . . . 175

    VII. THE PRESENT TEXT OF THE APOSTLES' CREED 187

# THE APOSTLES' CREED

A LECTURE

# THE APOSTLES' CREED

LIKE many another ancient document, the Apostles' Creed has had an interesting and complicated history. The form which we now have originated in western Europe, probably about the sixth century. But the present form is simply an expansion of a briefer creed which dates from a much earlier period and is commonly known among scholars as the "Old Roman Symbol." Our study of the Apostles' Creed, then, must concern itself largely with this Old Roman Symbol. Our sources for a knowledge of the older creed are fragmentary and scattered, but they have been subjected during recent years to the most careful and elaborate investigation and an immense amount of new light has been thrown upon them with the most gratifying results. Few better illustrations are to be found of the fruitfulness of modern historical and literary criticism than the recent advances in our knowledge along this line. Professor Caspari of Norway, who died in 1892, devoted years to the collection and investigation of the sources, and his minute and painstaking studies, published in a number of volumes, first brought the matter upon a genuinely scientific basis.¹ His work has been taken up more recently by Professor Kattenbusch of Tübingen, who has published a large work in two volumes, the first volume being devoted chiefly to the reconstruction of the text, and the second to the origin and interpretation both of the older symbol and of the present creed.² Kattenbusch's work is of a most exhaustive character, but it leaves many important questions unanswered, and I am convinced will have to be corrected at many points, particularly in connection with the origin, the purpose, and the historical interpretation of the Old Roman Symbol. A great many more or less elaborate pamphlets appeared in Germany a few years ago in connection with the controversy touching the use of the Apostles' Creed in the services of the church. Most of them are of a practical character and few of any scientific value, but the lecture of Professor Harnack,³ which gave rise to the con-

[1] Caspari's principal works upon the subject are *Ungedruckte, unbeachtete und wenig beachtete Quellen zur Geschichte des Taufsymbols und der Glaubensregel*: in three volumes, 1866, 1869, 1875, Christiania; and *Alte und neue Quellen zur Geschichte des Taufsymbols und der Glaubensregel*, Christiania, 1879.

[2] *Das apostolische Symbol: seine Entstehung, sein geschichtlicher Sinn, seine ursprüngliche Stellung im Kultus und in der Theologie der Kirche*. Bd. I: *Die Grundgestalt des Taufsymbols*, Leipzig, 1894; Bd. II: *Verbreitung und Bedeutung des Taufsymbols*, 1900.

[3] *Das apostolische Glaubensbekenntniss, ein geschichtlicher Bericht, nebst einem Nachwort*, Berlin, 1892; English translation by Mrs.

troversy, is an interesting and suggestive sketch of the origin and history of the creed, and the pamphlet of Professor Zahn [1] contains much material of value. Hahn's *Bibliothek der Symbole und Glaubensregeln der alten Kirche*, which appeared in a third and greatly improved edition in 1897, is indispensable to any one who wishes to make a study of the Old Roman Symbol and the Apostles' Creed, or indeed of any of the creeds of the early church. It is the most complete collection we have of the texts of ancient creeds both public and private, but it needs to be used with caution, as its texts are not always to be relied upon, and it should be tested in every case by Kattenbusch.[2]

Humphry Ward in the *Nineteenth Century* for July 1893. The little book by H. B. Swete (*The Apostles' Creed: its Relation to Primitive Christianity*, London, 1894) is in the main a defence of the primitive character of the creed over against Harnack.

Harnack has written upon one or another phase of the subject in numerous periodicals. His admirable summary in Herzog's Encyclopædia, third edition (s. v. *Das apostolische Symbol*) and his *Chronologie der alt-christlichen Litteratur*, Bd. I, S. 524 seq., should also be referred to, as well as his convenient collection of illustrative matter from the literature of the first two centuries in the appendix to the third edition of Hahn's *Bibliothek der Symbole und Glaubensregeln der alten Kirche*, Breslau, 1897.

[1] *Das apostolische Symbolum. Eine Skizze seiner Geschichte und eine Prüfung seines Inhalts*, Erlangen and Leipzig, 1893; English translation under the title *The Articles of the Apostles' Creed*, by A. E. Burn, London 1899.

Burn is himself the author of a recent work (*An Introduction to the Creeds and to the Te Deum*, London, 1899) which deals in part with the origin and history of the Apostles' Creed, and contains some new material.

[2] An elaborate conspectus of the literature upon the Apostles'

I have said that a briefer creed, commonly known as the Old Roman Symbol, underlies our present Apostles' Creed. From a work by Rufinus of Aquileia, written about 400 A.D., we learn that that symbol was in use in the church of Rome in the fourth century and a comparison of Rufinus' work with a letter of Marcellus of Ancyra, written some sixty years earlier, shows that the symbol at that time ran as follows: "I believe in God the Father almighty and in Christ Jesus his only begotten son our Lord, who was born of the Holy Spirit and Mary the Virgin, was crucified under Pontius Pilate and buried, on the third day rose from the dead, ascended into heaven, sitteth on the right hand of the Father, from whence he cometh to judge quick and dead; and in Holy Spirit, holy church, remission of sins, resurrection of flesh."[1]

This symbol, with the exception of two or three phrases, can be traced back to the latter part of the second century, our earliest witnesses to its existence being Tertullian of North Africa[2] and his older contemporary Irenæus of Southern Gaul.[3] There is some difficulty in reconstructing the exact text of the symbol as known to them.

Creed both old and new is given by Kattenbusch, I., p. 1 seq. and II., p. 729 seq. and 967 seq.

[1] Upon the text of the Old Roman Symbol in the fourth century, see p. 39 seq.
[2] See p. 47 seq.   [3] See p. 48 seq.

Many scholars maintain that it was the same as that known to Rufinus, but I think it can be shown that the phrases "only begotten" after "Christ Jesus," "of the Holy Spirit" after "born," "forgiveness of sins," and very likely also the article on the church, and possibly the phrase "our Lord" after "Christ Jesus his Son" were not a part of it in their time, so that it ran then substantially: "I believe in God the Father almighty and in Christ Jesus his son, who was born of Mary the Virgin, was crucified under Pontius Pilate and buried, on the third day rose from the dead, ascended into heaven, sitteth on the right hand of the Father, from whence he cometh to judge quick and dead; and in Holy Spirit, resurrection of flesh."[1]

I have said that Irenæus and Tertullian are our earliest witnesses to the existence of this symbol. It is true that some scholars think they can trace it still further back, finding evidences that it was already in use in Rome when Marcion came thither, and that it was known to Justin Martyr and even to some of the apostolic fathers. But after a very careful study of all our sources for a knowledge of Marcion's career and of the entire pre-Irenæan literature I am unable to find a single trace of the existence of our creed or of any similar creed before the time of Irenæus. It is

[1] On the original text of the Old Roman Symbol, see p. 84 seq.

true that many of the phrases which occur in the creed are common in the earliest fathers, but that proves nothing. It has been altogether too common to assume a knowledge of the creed wherever one of its phrases, or even phraseology remotely resembling any part of it has been found, as if the framer of the creed was himself the author of all its statements and did not rather gather them together from the common Christian thought and language of the day. Certainly a creed could hardly have hoped to find general acceptance which contained new and unfamiliar phraseology from beginning to end. In the complete absence of statements implying the existence of any creed whatever, there should be found at least such a collocation of creedal phrases and in such a connection as to make a creedal origin probable. It is not enough, as some have thought, to show that there is no conclusive evidence against the existence of the creed before the middle of the second century. The mere fact that it existed in 175 A.D. does not warrant us in pushing it back fifty or seventy-five years further unless there is positive evidence of an affirmative character. But as a matter of fact not simply is no such evidence forthcoming, there are on the contrary not a few indications of an opposite character. I cannot go into the details of the matter in this lecture. I may simply remark that the elaborate account of the rite of baptism which Justin Martyr gives in his first Apology makes decidedly against the use of a creed in Rome in his time, and the absence of any reference to a creed in the *Didache*, which has so much to say about pre-baptismal instruction, is conclusive proof that none was used in the part of the church to which the *Didache* belongs in the first quarter of the second century.[1]

Tertullian and Irenæus, then, are our earliest witnesses to the existence of a creed. Their testimony carries us back some years beyond 175 A.D., but not beyond the middle of the century. It would seem, in fact, that the creed known as the Old Roman Symbol must have originated between 150 and 175, a time when there was every reason for the formation of some creedal statement to guard against the misconceptions of Christianity which were widely prevalent and were causing serious trouble. It would seem, still further, that it must have originated in Rome, whence the other churches of the west certainly derived it. In Rome we can trace its existence as far back as 150–175, while there is no certain proof of any similar creed in any part of the east until well on in the third century. At this point I am glad to find myself in agreement with Kattenbusch, who maintains the Roman origin of the

[1] On the date of the Old Roman Symbol, see p. 46 seq.

creed over against the older view of Caspari that it took its rise in the east.[1]

The authorship of the Old Roman Symbol and the exact occasion of its composition we do not know, but it is quite clear that it was designed as a baptismal confession — a form of words in which the convert should declare his faith.[2] It seems natural enough now to use such a confession, but when one realizes the original Christian custom, the existence of the confession seems very strange. Peter at Pentecost said to his converts simply "Repent and be baptized." In the *Didache* only ethical instruction is given the candidate for baptism; and we learn from other sources that it was common in many quarters in the primitive church for the converts simply to pledge themselves at the time of baptism to commit no murder or theft or other crime and to live as became a follower of Christ.[3]

How, then, are we to account for the existence in the late second century of an elaborate baptismal confession in which all the emphasis is on belief and not a word is said about conduct? We do not need to search long in the literature of the second century to find an adequate answer.

---

[1] On the place of composition of the Old Roman Symbol, see p. 101 seq.

[2] Cf. *Irenæus*, I., 9, 4; 10, 1; and Tertullian, *De Corona*, 3.

[3] Cf., e. g., Pliny's *Epistle to Trajan*, No. 96 (97); and Hippolytus, *Phil.*, IX. 10.

Before the middle of that century there were Christians who were preaching views which most of the disciples regarded as the worst of heresies; views which appeared to be thoroughly heathen in their character and which it seemed that every true Christian believer must repudiate if he would remain true to Christ. Up to this time it had apparently been taken for granted that all converts from heathenism in receiving Christian baptism and casting in their lot with the disciples of Christ, would inevitably renounce all heathen errors opposed to the teaching of Christ and the spirit of the gospel. But it was becoming manifest in the second century that the assumption was unfounded, that there were many Christians who were bringing over with them into the church views about God and the world and Christ which seemed absolutely destructive of the Christian faith and life. And so the custom arose of inquiring, when new converts wished to be baptized, whether they renounced the false and pernicious ideas of the heathen and heretics, and it was apparently in order to insure such renunciation that the positive statement of faith which we know as the Old Roman Symbol was framed, and all candidates for baptism in Rome were required to learn it by heart and repeat it in the most solemn manner at the time of their baptism. At this point I must confess myself to be out of agreement with the opinion commonly prevalent among recent scholars, including even Harnack and Kattenbusch. Most of them regard the Old Roman Symbol as a positive statement of the Christian faith framed quite independently of existing errors and with a primarily evangelistic or missionary purpose. This opinion I was compelled some years ago to abandon, and continued study has only confirmed me in my abandonment of it. The structure of the creed, its omissions as well as its assertions, the date at which it arose and the contrast between its use at baptism and the earlier custom, when the church had hardly begun to be troubled by false teaching and was chiefly interested in evangelism — all point in the same direction, and seem to me to make it certain that the Old Roman Symbol, like most of the great historic creeds, arose as a protest against error.[1] It is in the light, then, of the errors against which it was directed that it must be interpreted.[2] But it is to be noticed that the Old Roman Symbol is not a general statement of the faith of the Christians of the second century over against all the errors of the day. There are many essential elements in their faith which have no place in the symbol, and there were not a few common errors

---

[1] Upon the purpose of the Old Roman Symbol, see p. 106 seq.
[2] For a detailed interpretation of the Old Roman Symbol, see p. 108 seq.

which are passed by without notice. The symbol, in fact, as is quite evident, is in the main a simple enlargement of the baptismal formula, and it is concerned chiefly to state the true Christian faith touching the persons into whose names the convert is baptized.

The movement which was making most trouble in Rome at the time the Old Roman Symbol was framed was that of Marcion, the would-be Pauline reformer. Marcion's radical Paulinism led him to repudiate not only the law but the law-giver; and so he drew a sharp distinction between the God of the Jews and the God of the Christians, and denied that the latter was the creator and ruler of the world revealed in the Old Testament — denied, in fact, that he had anything to do with making and governing the material universe. Marcion thus cut the root of the belief in providence upon which Jesus laid so great stress, and which is really essential to genuine and healthy Christian living.

It was over against this error that the first article in the Old Roman symbol seems to have been framed: "I believe in God the Father almighty." The word in the original Greek — παντοκράτωρ — means not "almighty" but "all controlling" or "all governing," the reference being to God as the one who holds and controls and governs the universe. The connection then makes it clear that the word Father meant "Father of the universe," Father being used in the sense of Author or Maker as it was commonly used by the Christians of the second century. Thus when the early Christians uttered the first article of the creed they were not asserting their faith in the Father as the first person of the Trinity, or in God as the loving and merciful Father of men, whom Christ preached; but in God the creator and ruler of the universe, a belief which is Christian, but not distinctively so, for it is much older than Christ and has always been shared by many quite without the circle of Christian influence.

The second article of the creed—the article on Christ—is not simply the most elaborate but the most striking part of it. It is significant as well for its omissions as for its assertions. Nothing is said about the baptism of Christ, of which so much is made in the gospels and which we know was emphasized in many quarters in the second century; nothing is said of Christ's teaching, or of his works of mercy and of power; nothing of his fulfilment of messianic prophecy, upon which all the early missionaries, whether addressing Jews or gentiles, laid the very greatest stress, upon which in fact they chiefly based their claim that Christ was a messenger sent from God; nothing is said of the salvation brought by Jesus and nothing of the purpose of his life or death. It does not help matters to say that the brevity of the creed required the omission of these things, for they are of primary importance, and some of them certainly occupy a far larger place in the New Testament and in the preaching of the missionaries of the first and second centuries than some of the things that are mentioned, than the virgin birth, for instance, and the ascension. And the insertion of the word " buried " after " crucified " shows that brevity was not the only consideration. Evidently the second article was not intended as a summary, even of the briefest character, of what the Christians of the second century believed about Christ. It was rather a statement designed particularly to meet certain specific difficulties and errors. Among the teachings of Marcion which were most offensive to Christians in general was the assertion that Jesus Christ is not the son of the creator and ruler of the world—the God of the Old Testament—but of another being altogether, who was entirely unknown until the coming of Christ. One can hardly resist the conclusion that the author of the Old Roman Symbol had this in mind when he declared that the Jesus Christ into whose name the convert is baptized is the son of the creator and ruler of the universe mentioned in the first article.

The sentences which immediately follow seem to be primarily intended as an assertion of the reality of Christ's earthly life. He was born of a woman—the Virgin Mary—a birth which Marcion absolutely denied; he was crucified, buried, rose again, and ascended. The docetism of Marcion and the Gnostics and many other Christians of the second century is familiar to all of us, their denial of the reality of Christ's earthly life, which took the form either of a denial of the material reality of his body or of the assertion that the spiritual heavenly Christ, and the man Jesus, were two distinct beings, so that it could not be said that Christ himself was crucified and buried and rose again. The creed in asserting that *Christ Jesus* was born and was crucified and buried and rose again, and that it was the crucified and buried one that ascended to heaven, repudiates in the most explicit terms the whole docetic conception.

The omission of the baptism is also worth noting in this connection. Of the baptism many of the docetic sects made a great deal, holding that it was at the time of the baptism that the heavenly Christ came down upon the man Jesus to abide with him during his public ministry, and to leave him again just before his crucifixion. It was found difficult in view of the account of the baptism in the gospels to meet the arguments of the docetists and so the tendency arose to minimize the baptism, and the result was that it found an entrance into none of the historic creeds. As the baptism received less emphasis the virgin birth received proportionately more. The belief in the virgin birth, though certainly not common in the earliest days, had become widespread before the end of the first century, as is shown by the gospels of Matthew and Luke and by the epistles of Ignatius, and was a part of the general faith of the church before the Old Roman Symbol was framed. At the same time the interest underlying the statement "born of Mary the Virgin" in the symbol, must be recognized to have been not the uniqueness of Christ's birth so much as the reality of it. What the convert was asked to do was to declare his belief that Christ was born of a woman, and this doubtless he might have done in the words of the original symbol even had he not believed that Christ's birth was different from that of other men. But the subsequent insertion of the words "of the Holy Spirit" marks a change of interest and of emphasis. Just when the words were added we do not know, probably at the latest not long after the beginning of the third century. They were, of course, not supposed to add anything new to the creed, for the phrase "born of Mary the Virgin" seemed to carry with it by implication the agency of the Holy Spirit as recounted in Matthew and Luke. At the same time their addition does indicate a desire to emphasize the divineness of Christ's origin, which seemed to the original framers of the creed in less need of emphasis than the reality of his humanity.[1]

I spoke a few moments ago of Marcion's denial of the identity of the God of the Jews and the God of the Christians, and of his assertion that Jesus Christ is the son, not of the former but of the latter, not of the creator and ruler of the world, but of a God entirely unknown until the coming of Christ. I spoke also of his docetism, which took all reality out of the earthly life of Christ. Another Marcionitic tenet which gave widespread offence, and was regarded by Christians in general as peculiarly dangerous, was the denial of the last judgment. Marcion conceived of the Christian God, the God of redemption revealed by Christ, as pure love and mercy, and denied that he or his son, Jesus Christ, would judge any one. In the article on the judgment in the Old Roman Symbol, joined as it is to the session at the right hand of the Father, the Marcionitic position is repudiated in the most emphatic way. Christ will come again from the right hand of the Father, that is, with his authority and as his agent, to judge the living and the dead.

The article on the Holy Spirit which follows the article on the judgment was not called forth by any anti-heathen or anti-heretical interest, for

[1] See p. 122 seq.

neither heathen nor heretics had any difficulty in believing in one or in many divine spirits. It is noticeable that the creed does not say "One Holy Spirit" or even "The Holy Spirit," at least not in the best text, but simply πνεῦμα ἅγιον without article or qualifying phrase. Evidently the mention of the Holy Spirit in the creed was due simply to its occurrence in the baptismal formula upon which the creed was based.

I have said that the creed is an enlargement of the baptismal formula, and it is commonly, I may say universally assumed that it is an enlargement of the formula found in Matt. xxviii. 19: "Into the name of the Father and of the Son and of the Holy Spirit." But I think it can be shown, though I cannot stop to discuss the matter here, that the formula upon which it is based was rather "Into the name of God and of Jesus Christ and of the Holy Spirit" a formula which, as I think it can also be shown, is older than the triune formula of Matthew. It is found in 2 Cor. xiii. 13 as a formula of benediction, and its use in Rome in the middle of the second century in connection with baptism is testified to by Justin Martyr, who throws more light than any other father upon the conditions existing in Rome just before the time when the creed originated.[1]

[1] Upon the baptismal formula and its relation to the Old Roman Symbol, see p. 175 seq.

But this conclusion is in line with a conclusion which may be drawn independently from the creed itself, and that is that in the creed the convert declared his faith not in the three persons of the Trinity — God the Father, God the Son, and God the Holy Spirit — but in God, and in the historic person Jesus Christ, and in the Holy Spirit. Neither the deity of Christ nor his pre-existence was referred to in the original symbol, nor did that symbol contain any reference to an incarnation. For a creedal statement of Christ's pre-existence, deity, and incarnation the church had to wait until Nicæa.

In the declaration of belief in God the Father almighty and in his Son Jesus Christ and in the Holy Spirit the content of the baptismal formula is fully reproduced. What follows is not based upon the baptismal formula, but is added apparently in order to repudiate other particularly troublesome errors.

The article on the resurrection of the flesh, phrased as it is with the emphasis upon the flesh, would seem to be a protest against the Marcionitic denial of the salvability of the flesh, a denial which was regarded as one of the worst and most dangerous of all heresies in the second century. The church at large was not satisfied with Paul's doctrine of a spiritual body, which the Marcionites and many of the Gnostics made their own, but insisted upon the resurrection of this very flesh, with all its particles intact and unchanged, in order to prepare the believer for the earthly millennial kingdom which Christ was to return and establish. The original significance of this article is somewhat obscured in our English translation of it: "Resurrection of the body." The word body, of course, admits of the Pauline interpretation, the resurrection namely of a spiritual body which amounts to no more than personal immortality. But in its original form the fleshly character of the resurrection was asserted and even emphasized, and so the article had a distinctly, though not of course consciously anti-Pauline meaning."[1]

One of the most interesting articles in the creed is the "forgiveness of sins." It was apparently not a part of the original symbol, for neither Irenæus nor Tertullian mentions it; but it seems to have been added soon after 200, and I cannot resist the conclusion that it was inserted with a reference to the controversy which was then going on in Rome over the question whether the forgiveness of post-baptismal sins is possible. So that while the statement itself is general and preserves what has always been regarded as one of the most precious and fundamental truths of the gospel of Christ, it would seem to have been put into the creed with a

[1] On this article, see p. 164 seq.

distinctly hierarchical reference, to commit the convert to the Catholic principle of absolution, upon which Bishop Callixtus of Rome took his stand over against the earlier principle that the church is a community of saints and that there is no absolution but only excommunication for those who commit mortal sins after baptism.[1]

The article on the church may not have been in the original symbol, as Irenæus does not refer to it and Tertullian does not give it in his reproductions of the creed. If it did actually constitute a part of the original text it may possibly have been intended as a protest against the Gnostics' denial of the holiness of the church at large and their assertion that only they themselves, an elect few within the church, are really holy and really saved.

On the other hand, if the article was added, as it perhaps was, early in the third century, it must have been a fruit of the controversy just referred to touching the forgiveness of post-baptismal sins, and connected as it is with the article on the forgiveness of sins it must have been intended, in that case, to assert that though the church receives back into communion excommunicated offenders, and so is composed of sinners as well as saints, yet the church is a holy church.[2]

This completes the interpretation of the Old

---

[1] See p. 155 seq.   [2] See p. 161 seq.

Roman Symbol. But our present Apostles' Creed contains other clauses not found in the older symbol. Before attempting to interpret them let us look at the origin of the enlarged creed.[1] An examination of the various western texts given by Hahn and Kattenbusch shows that three general types of creed may be distinguished: first the Italian type, which is nearest to the Old Roman Symbol and reproduces it with only slight variations; secondly the North African type, which reproduces the Old Roman Symbol with certain common and stereotyped additions; and thirdly the west European type, which is farthest from the Old Roman symbol and is characterized by greater freedom and variety than either of the other types, additions being made apparently to meet local needs and without much regard to the forms in use in neighboring churches.[2] The general difference in these three types is just what we should expect. In Italy Rome was dominant and it was natural that its creed should be used with few changes. In

[1] See Kattenbusch, II., p. 759 seq., for an elaborate discussion of this question.

[2] See Kattenbusch, I., p. 194 seq. Harnack distinguishes four types (Italian, North African, Spanish, and Gallic), and assigns our present text to the last (see his article in the third edition of Herzog, p. 746, and cf. Kattenbusch, II., p. 778). That there are some characteristic differences between the known Spanish and Gallic creeds is true, but in the present uncertainty as to the exact home of many western texts we can hardly distinguish between two western types with the same sharpness as between the Italian, North African, and Western.

Africa the church of Carthage had paramount influence, and it was natural that while additions to the Roman symbol should be more freely made than in Italy they should all conform closely to the Carthaginian type. In western Europe, on the other hand, there was no central authority and no dominating church or bishop. The west felt the influence both of Rome and of North Africa, but the several churches developed with considerable freedom and independence, and so we should expect to find variety in the texts of their creeds, the only common element being the Roman original upon which they were all built.

Our present Apostles' Creed belongs evidently to the western type. One of the additions which it contains (descended into Hades) appeared first in Italy; another (eternal life) in North Africa, but both are found also a little later in the texts of western Europe, and there are others which are found first in those texts; as for instance: "creatorem coeli et terrae;" "qui conceptus est;" "passus et mortuus;" "Dei omnipotentis" (in the article on the session); "catholicam" (with church); and "communionem sanctorum." Indeed only in western texts are all the additions to the Old Roman Symbol found before our Apostles' Creed appears in exactly its present form. There can thus be practically no doubt that the present form originated in western Europe even though we cannot fix the exact time or place of its formation.¹

But though our present creed is of the western type, it is not the fullest and richest form of that type. It is simply one of a number of forms, some of which are even more elaborate than it. For instance, we find in other western texts "Deum et Dominum" with "Jesum Christum;" "vivus" with "resurrexit;" "victor" with "ascendit in coelos;" "omnium" with "peccatorum;" "per baptismum" with "remissionem;" "hujus" with "carnis," and so on. Moreover the additions which are found in our present text cannot be pronounced superior to those that occur in other texts, nor does a single principle underlie them, so that they can be said to belong naturally together. There seems in fact to have been no reason in the nature of the case why other additions instead of these might not have been permanently adopted. The present form is not the one legitimate and final result of the development of the Old Roman Symbol.² It is simply

¹ The common and probably the correct opinion is that the present form of the Apostles' Creed originated in Gaul (cf. Harnack's article in Herzog). In the first volume of his work (p. 196 seq.) Kattenbusch says that we have no means of determining the place of its origin, beyond the fact that it belongs to Western Europe, but in the second volume (p. 790 seq.) he gives reasons for thinking that it may have originated in the province of Burgundy. Burn (Introduction to the Creeds, p. 221 seq.) assigns it to Rome, but without sufficient reason (cf. Kattenbusch, II., p. 784 seq.).

² Cf. Kattenbusch, I., p. 195 seq., and also II., p. 779, where

one of the many enlarged forms of it, and why it persisted rather than one of the others, or in other words why it rather than one of the others became in the early middle ages the creed of Rome and so finally the creed of the whole western church, we do not know. Possibly it was the form, among the many current in the west, which happened to be in use at the Frankish court in the eighth century when the Franks were beginning to dominate Rome.[1]

The way in which this western form of the Old Roman Symbol became itself the baptismal creed of the Roman church and was handed down to subsequent centuries as the Apostles' Creed, and the hereditary symbol of Rome, is very interesting, though it has not yet been fully cleared up. We know that in the fifth or sixth century the Old Roman Symbol fell into disuse in Rome and the so-called Nicene creed became the chief baptismal symbol of the church of that city.[2] Just why this happened is uncertain. Possibly it was because of the dominating influence of the Eastern empire; possibly because of the Arianism of the Goths and the Lombards, against which it seemed important to guard the convert. At any rate, the Nicene

he answers the criticisms of Harnack in the third edition of Herzog's Encyclopædia, s. v. *Apostolisches Symbol*.

[1] Cf. Kattenbusch, II., p. 967.

[2] See Caspari, *Quellen*, II., p. 114, note 88; and compare Kattenbusch, II., p. 796 seq.

creed continued in use for some two centuries or more and by that time the Old Roman Symbol which had been exclusively employed until the fifth or sixth century seems to have been generally though not altogether forgotten. Meanwhile, in the eighth or ninth century, our present form of the Apostles' Creed came into use in Rome in connection with baptism and ultimately crowded out the Nicene Creed altogether.[1] The process by which this second displacement was brought about is even more obscure than the first. We only know that the enlarged form was current among the Franks in the eighth century, and as Frankish influence began at that time to be strongly felt in Rome, and as the pope was drawing ever further away from the Eastern empire and was beginning to form an alliance with the Franks, it may well be that the substitution of the present Apostles' Creed for the Nicene was simply a part of the general papal policy.

But there is still more to be told in this romantic chapter of symbolics. The Old Roman Symbol which was framed in the second century was regarded before the end of that century as an apostolic rule of faith, as a standard and norm of

---

[1] See Caspari, III., pp. 201 seq., 226; and compare Kattenbusch, II., pp. 794 seq., 967. Just when this displacement was accomplished we do not know. In the ninth century both the Nicene and the present Apostles' Creed were in use in Rome in connection with baptism. See Kattenbusch, II., p. 800.

apostolic truth possessing equal authority with the apostolic scripture canon.[1] In course of time this belief in its general apostolic origin was made definite and vivid by the ascription of the several articles of the creed to the several apostles, one article to each. This is found first in a work of the late fourth or early fifth century ascribed to Ambrose, in which it is said that the apostles gathered together after the ascension of Christ and published a symbol, which was made brief that it might be easily remembered, and which was composed of twelve sentences as there were twelve apostles. It is also said that this was the symbol which had been preserved in the church of Rome and that it was worse to add or subtract anything than in the case of the Apocalypse, for it was the work of twelve apostles, but the Apocalypse of only one.[2] When this legend arose we do not know. It was evidently due only to the desire to make the general belief in the apostolic origin of the symbol vivid and realistic. But now comes the striking part of the story. After the western creed had supplanted the Nicene creed in

---

[1] Cf., e. g., Tertullian's *De Praescriptione Haereticorum*.

[2] *Explanatio Symboli ad initiandos*, Migne, *Patr. Lat.*, xvii. 1155–59. Cf. also Rufinus (*Expositio Symboli*, chap. ii.), who says: "Being all therefore met together they [i. e., the apostles] composed this brief formulary of their future preaching, by gathering together into one what each thought." Upon the authorship of the *Explanatio Symboli ad initiandos*, see Kattenbusch, I., p. 84 seq., and upon the legend of Apostolic authorship, *ibid.*, II., p. 1 seq.

Rome, the legend which had attached in earlier days to the Old Roman Symbol attached itself to the new creed, and from that time until the fifteenth century it was believed that the creed in the form which we still use was the direct composition of the several apostles, each contributing his respective clause. The legend first appears attached to our present Apostles' Creed in a discourse of the early middle ages whose author, date, and place of composition are unknown. The passage containing the creed is given by Hahn (§ 42) and runs as follows: "On the tenth day after the ascension when the disciples were gathered for fear of the Jews, the Lord sent the promised Paraclete. And when he had come as a flaming fire and they were filled with the knowledge of all tongues they composed the symbol. Peter said: I believe in God the Father almighty, maker of heaven and earth. Andrew said: And in Jesus Christ his only Son, our Lord. James said: Who was conceived by the Holy Spirit, born of Mary the Virgin. John said: Suffered under Pontius Pilate, was crucified, dead, and buried. Thomas said: Descended into Hades, on the third day rose from the dead. James said: Ascended into heaven, sitteth at the right hand of God the Father almighty. Philip said: Thence he is about to come to judge quick and dead. Bartholomew said: I believe in the Holy Spirit. Matthew said:

Holy catholic church, communion of saints. Simon said: Remission of sins. Thaddæus said: Resurrection of the flesh. Matthias said: Life eternal."[1]

The truth of the legend was first questioned by Laurentius Valla in the fifteenth century,[2] and was finally given up by both Protestants and Roman Catholics, though the latter still claim for the creed apostolic authorship in a general sense.[3]

I have left myself little time to speak of the additions which distinguish the western creed — our present Apostles' Creed — from the Old Roman Symbol. Only four of them are of particular importance: "Descended into Hades"; the word "Catholic" in the article on the church; "Communion of saints," and "Life eternal."[4]

"Descended into Hades" first appears as a part of the Apostles' Creed in the version of the Aqui-

---

[1] On this text see Kattenbusch, I., p. 192, II., p. 777.

[2] At the Council of Florence, in 1438, where attempts were made to bring about a union of the Greek and Roman churches, the eastern theologians declared that the eastern church had no Apostles' Creed and knew nothing about such a creed. As a matter of fact, the Nicæno-Constantinopolitan creed had been the baptismal symbol of the Eastern church since the fifth century, and the Apostles' Creed was neither known nor used there. It was probably as a result of the discussions at this Council that Laurentius Valla threw doubt upon the truth of the legend concerning apostolic authorship which had grown up in the West but had never had a place in the East. See Kattenbusch, I., p. 1 seq.

[3] See the *Catechismus Romanus*, Caput I., Quaestio II.

[4] See p. 187 seq. for a discussion of all the articles and phrases that distinguish the present Apostles' Creed from the Old Roman Symbol.

leian symbol given by Rufinus, who distinctly says that it was not in the Roman symbol of his day, that is, 400 A. D. It appears occasionally in western texts of the next two or three centuries, including the text of our present Apostles' Creed. The purpose of its insertion in the creed we do not know. It was perhaps intended to emphasize the completeness of Christ's death over against the subtle docetism of the third and fourth centuries, which had resulted from the spread of the Logos christology, and which tended to confine the human nature of Christ to his material body, and so take away from his death all spiritual significance. But if this was the reason for the insertion of the article the reason had been forgotten in Aquileia when Rufinus wrote, for he finds in the words only a repetition of the statement that Christ was buried.

The article does not mean that Christ descended into hell, or the place of punishment for lost souls, but into the underworld, or abode of the dead. The belief that Christ thus descended into Hades between his death and resurrection is as old as the first century and all sorts of ideas had attached themselves to it, the commonest being that Christ had descended in order to preach to the dead, or in order to destroy the power of Satan. But the article as it stands in the creed has nothing to say about the purpose of the

Descent, and there is no reason to think that its author reflected particularly upon that purpose. He was interested apparently only in the fact.

The adjective "catholic" in the article on the church appears in the creed as early as the fourth century and was very common from the fifth century on. The addition of the word was very natural, as the phrase "Holy catholic church" was a current phrase. At the time when it was inserted in the creed it had already acquired an exclusive meaning and it was that meaning therefore which attached to it in the creed; belief being expressed not in the holy church universal, but in the particular institution which was known as the Catholic Church and was distinguished from all schismatic and heretical bodies, the orthodox catholic church which was in communion with the church of Rome. The common Protestant interpretation of the article in the creed, which makes it refer to the holy church universal, is therefore historically incorrect.

The article on the communion of saints is very obscure. It appears in various western texts of the fifth and following centuries, but why it was inserted and what it was intended to express we cannot be sure. The phrase was a common one in the west from the fifth century on. It was used sometimes to denote participation in sacred things, that is the sacraments, sometimes to denote communion with departed saints. And one or the other of these meanings probably attaches to the article in the creed. There is no sign that the article was intended to express the communion or fellowship of believers with each other, or that it was meant as a closer definition of the word "church," as we so commonly interpret it to-day.

The article "Eternal life" appears frequently in texts of the fourth and following centuries. The phrase needs no special interpretation. It was a most natural addition after the article on the resurrection and it is not necessary to seek for any particular occasion for its insertion. It supplies a lack in the Old Roman Symbol which must have been widely felt when the original polemic purpose of that symbol was forgotten. The earlier symbol closed abruptly with the resurrection of the flesh. The conclusion of the present creed is far more satisfactory and expresses far more adequately the Christian hope.

Before closing this lecture permit me to call attention briefly to three or four points suggested by the account I have given of the origin and early history of the creed. In the first place the Apostles' Creed is not a monument of the apostolic or early post-apostolic age. It belongs even in its earliest form to the age when the catholic spirit was beginning to displace the primitive spirit and when the interest in sound doctrine was beginning to crowd out the interest in the evangelization and salvation of the world. It is primarily a doctrinal and polemical creed, not an evangelistic or missionary symbol.

In the second place, belonging as it does to another age, it is very far from reproducing the original Christian gospel. There is nothing in it of the personal fatherhood of God; nothing of the Messiahship of Jesus; nothing of the kingdom of God; nothing of repentance and faith; nothing of love for God and one's neighbors; nothing of following Christ; nothing of the forgiveness of sin (at least in the original text). Moreover in its account of Christ's life it omits his baptism, which is emphasized by all the gospels; his works of mercy and power; his fulfilment of prophecy; his preaching and founding of the kingdom. While on the other hand it contains the virgin birth, which was believed at a comparatively early day, to be sure, but certainly did not constitute a part of the original preaching of the disciples.

In the third place not simply does the creed fail to reproduce the original Christian gospel in its true proportions and in some of its essential elements; it represents only a small part of the thinking even of the age which gave it birth and it omits much that was most essential in that thinking. Nothing is said in it about the pre-existence of Christ or about salvation through him; nothing about the nature of Christianity and the Christian life; nothing about the authority of the Old Testament; nothing about the coming kingdom; nothing about the life eternal, at least in the original text. Evidently it is not a summary of the faith of the church either of the second or of any other century.

In the fourth place, while we of to-day can repeat parts of it, probably not one of us can repeat the whole of it in the sense which was originally intended. The interpretation of creeds inevitably changes with time and the changed interpretation must be recognized as legitimate, or the historic creeds must be repudiated altogether.

Finally the great value of the creed above all other creeds which the church possesses is its emphasis upon the historic figure, Jesus Christ. We may well congratulate ourselves that the great heresy of the second century was the denial of the reality of Christ's humanity, for we owe to it a distinct and unequivocal statement of Christ's real manhood in a creed which for simplicity and compactness has never been surpassed, and which has been handed down through the centuries and has been reverenced by half of Christendom as the creed of the apostles themselves. Perhaps to it more than to anything else — more even than to the gospels, which were not widely read in the middle ages—we owe the fact that Jesus Christ is and always has been the object of the Christian's faith, and that his figure has never been completely lost even when the true gospel has been most overlaid with scholastic philosophy or with sacramentarianism and ecclesiasticism.

# CRITICAL NOTES

# CRITICAL NOTES

## I

### THE TEXT OF THE OLD ROMAN SYMBOL IN THE FOURTH CENTURY

THE most explicit and definite testimony which we have to the existence and form of the Old Roman Symbol is in Rufinus' *Expositio Symboli*,[1] which was written about 400 A.D. In this work, which is a commentary upon the creed as used in the church of Aquileia in Rufinus' time, the author gives the text of the Aquileian creed and points out its variations from the creed of the church of Rome. It is thus possible to reconstruct the latter as it existed in Rufinus' day, at least so far as its substance goes. It is evident that Rufinus calls attention to all the variations that are of any importance, but there may have been differences of mere verbiage which he says nothing about. His creed is given by Hahn, § 36, with the additions to the Roman creed indicated by italics. Compare also Kattenbusch, I. p. 60 seq.

---

[1] Migne, *Patr. Lat.*, Vol. XXI., col. 335–386; English translation in the Nicene and Post-Nicene Fathers, 2nd series, Vol. III., p. 541 seq.

About the year 337 A.D. Marcellus of Ancyra wrote a letter to Julius, Bishop of Rome, which has been preserved by Epiphanius, *Haer.*, 72. The letter was written by Marcellus to defend himself from charges of heresy which had been preferred against him, and contains a creed, which is given by Hahn, § 17 (cf. also Kattenbusch, I. p. 64 seq.). Marcellus does not say where he got this creed. Indeed, he introduces it abruptly without preface of any kind. But it is clear that he did not compose it for the occasion as a summary of his own personal faith, for it has no direct bearing upon the questions at issue between him and his opponents, and one might accept the whole of it and still take either side in the controversy. The only plausible explanation of the insertion of the creed without preface or description is that it was the recognized creed of the church of Rome, and that Marcellus hoped to establish his orthodoxy to the satisfaction of the Roman bishop by declaring his acceptance of it in full. And a comparison of it with the Roman creed as found in Rufinus confirms this conclusion, for the two agree almost verbatim; the only important differences being the omission of πατέρα in the first article of Marcellus' creed and the addition of ζωὴν αἰώνιον at the end.

Three other witnesses to the text of the Old Roman Symbol are found in three manuscripts of the early middle ages, one Greek and two Latin, the first known as the Psalterium Æthelstani, the second as the Codex Laudianus, and the third called by Kattenbusch the Codex Swainsonii, because discovered by Swainson. (See Hahn, §§ 18, 20, 23 ; and Kattenbusch, I. p. 64 seq.) The manuscripts say nothing about the source from whence they draw the creed, but the agreement is so complete between the three texts and the text of the Old Roman Symbol given by Rufinus that there can be no doubt that they are reproducing the same symbol. These five witnesses enable us to reconstruct with considerable accuracy the text of the Old Roman Symbol as it existed in the fourth century. The Psalterium Æthelstani, the Codex Laudianus and the Codex Swainsonii agree with Rufinus over against Marcellus in having πατέρα (*patrem*) in the first article and in omitting ζωὴν αἰώνιον in the last. The text of Epiphanius is very corrupt just at the point where the letter of Marcellus is quoted, so that the variations may be due to textual errors in Epiphanius; or Marcellus, who had very likely first seen the Roman creed during a recent visit in Rome and now quoted it from memory, may have misquoted it at the two points in question. At any rate it may be regarded as certain that the phrase ζωὴν αἰώνιον was not in the Old Roman Symbol at the time Marcellus wrote, for the three later witnesses all omit it, and it is inconceivable that it should have been in the creed originally and have been later omitted and then found a place again in the enlarged form of the creed which we now know as the Apostles' creed. As the phrase had a place in all the eastern creeds of Marcellus' day it was easy for it to slip in inadvertently when he quoted the Roman symbol. So far as the omission of πατέρα is concerned it is possible, of course, that the word did not belong to the creed when Marcellus wrote, but was added before the time of Rufinus. But, as will be shown later (see p. 99), it is altogether probable that it was in the original text of the creed and its omission, therefore, was doubtless due to an oversight on the part of Marcellus himself or of some scribe. We may assume then that the Old Roman Symbol ran substantially as follows in the time of Marcellus and Rufinus:

πιστεύω εἰς Θεὸν πατέρα[1] παντοκράτορα· καὶ εἰς Χριστὸν Ἰησοῦν, τὸν[2] υἱὸν αὐτοῦ τὸν μονογενῆ, τὸν κύριον ἡμῶν, τὸν γεννηθέντα ἐκ πνεύματος ἁγίου καὶ Μαρίας τῆς παρθένου, τὸν ἐπὶ Ποντίου Πιλάτου σταυρωθέντα καὶ ταφέντα,[3] τῇ τρίτῃ ἡμέρᾳ ἀναστάντα ἐκ[4] νεκρῶν, ἀναβάντα εἰς τοὺς οὐρανούς, καθήμενον[5] ἐν δεξιᾷ τοῦ πατρός, ὅθεν ἔρχεται κρῖναι[6]

---

[1] Marcellus omits πατέρα. [2] Psalterium Æthelstani omits τόν.
[3] Marcellus has καὶ before τῇ τρίτῃ ἡμέρᾳ. [4] Marcellus has τῶν before νεκρῶν. [5] Marcellus has καὶ before καθήμενον. [6] Marcellus

ζῶντας καὶ νεκρούς· καὶ εἰς πνεῦμα ἅγιον,⁷ ἁγίαν ἐκκλησίαν, ἄφεσιν ἁμαρτιῶν, σαρκὸς ἀνάστασιν.⁸

Credo in Deum patrem omnipotentem;¹ et in Christum Jesum,² filium ejus unicum,³ dominum nostrum,⁴ qui natus est de Spiritu Sancto et⁵ Maria virgine, qui sub Pontio Pilato crucifixus est⁶ et sepultus, tertia die resurrexit a mortuis, ascendit in coelos,⁷ sedet⁸ ad dexteram Patris, unde⁹ venturus est judicare vivos et ¹⁰ mortuos; et in Spiritum Sanctum,¹¹ sanctam ecclesiam, remissionem peccatorum, carnis resurrectionem.

The question suggests itself which of these two texts, the Latin or the Greek, is the original and which the translation. The one is a very careful and literal reproduction of the other. The order of the words is preserved almost unchanged from beginning to end, and the only important difference is in the portion dealing with the career of Christ, where the Latin has relative clauses and the Greek participial. But even in this part the order of the words is identical in the two versions.

has κρίνειν. ⁷ Marcellus has τὸ ἅγιον πνεῦμα. ⁸ Marcellus adds ζωὴν αἰώνιον.

¹ Rufinus has *in Deo patre omnipotente*. ² Rufinus has *in Christo Jesu;* Codex Swainsonii has *in Jesum Christum*. ³ Rufinus has *unico filio ejus*. ⁴ Rufinus has *Domino nostro*. ⁵ Rufinus has *ex*. ⁶ Rufinus has *crucifixus sub Pontio Pilato*. ⁷ Codex Laudianus has *in coelis*. ⁸ Codex Swainsonii has *sedit*. ⁹ Rufinus has *inde*. ¹⁰ Cod. Swains. has *ac*. ¹¹ Rufinus has *et in Spiritu Sancto*. I have noted all the variations except the impossible case-endings of the Codex Laudianus, which are evidently due to ignorance of Latin syntax, as, e. g., *ad dextera patris*.

A careful comparison of the two in detail seems to show that the Greek and not the Latin was the original and that for the following reasons :

1. The words παντοκράτωρ and μονογενής are much more pregnant and expressive than the Latin words *omnipotens* and *unicus*, and are more likely to have been the originals than vice versa. Early Christian literature shows that παντοκράτωρ was commonly translated by *omnipotens* and μονογενής by *unicus*, while the more general Latin words would hardly suggest the rarer and more special Greek words.

2. The position of the phrases "under Pontius Pilate" and "on the third day" is emphatic in the Greek, but not in the Latin. On the other hand the phrase "into heaven" has the position of emphasis in the Latin but not in the Greek. We can see that there was good reason for emphasizing the former phrases, to make the time explicit, but there can hardly have been a reason for emphasizing the last phrase, for whither should Christ have ascended if not into heaven? It is unlikely that in all these cases the translation, while following exactly the order of the original, should be more expressive than that original.

3. Ὅθεν ἔρχεται κρῖναι ζῶντας καὶ νεκρούς is good Greek, but the corresponding clause *unde venturus est judicare vivos et mortuos* is not good Latin. It is true that the construction does occur

occasionally in Latin under the influence of the Greek, but the natural Latin expression would be *unde ad judicandos* (or *judicaturus*) *vivos et mortuos venturus est*, and it is certainly unlikely that the translation, while agreeing so closely with the construction and the order of words of the original, should be truer to the genius of the language than the original upon which it was based.

4. Finally, as will appear later, the Old Roman Symbol was probably composed in Rome not far from the middle of the second century, and at that time Greek not Latin was the language in commonest use among the Christians of Rome.

In view of all these considerations we may regard as well founded the conclusion of Caspari, Kattenbusch and most other scholars, that the Greek text is the original and the Latin the translation (cf. Caspari, *Quellen*, III. pp. 74 seq., 139 seq., and Kattenbusch, I. p. 67 seq.).

## II

### The Date of the Old Roman Symbol

The testimony of Marcellus of Ancyra carries us back beyond the middle of the fourth century. Possible traces of the existence of the Symbol testified to by him and by Rufinus are found in the third century in the writings of Dionysius of Rome, of Novatian and of Hippolytus (see Kattenbusch, II. p. 354-372), and Cyprian of Carthage refers explicitly to a symbol in use both in Carthage and in Rome, but he indicates its contents only in part. Thus in *Ep.* 69 he says " Quod si aliquis illud opponit ut dicat, eandem Novatianum legem tenere, quam catholica ecclesia teneat, eodem symbolo quo et nos baptizare, eundem nosse Deum patrem, eundem Filium Christum, eundem spiritum sanctum, ac propter hoc usurpare eum potestatem baptizandi posse, quod videatur interrogatione baptismi a nobis non discrepare, sciat quisquis hoc opponendum putat, primum non esse unam nobis et schismaticis symboli legem neque eandem interrogationem. Nam cum dicunt: Credis in remissionem peccatorum et vitam aeternam per sanctam ecclesiam? mentiuntur interrogatione, quando non habeant ecclesiam"; and in *Ep.* 70: " Sed et ipsa interrogatio, quae fit in baptismo, testis est veritatis. Nam cum dicimus: Credis in vitam aeternam et remissionem peccatorum per sanctam ecclesiam? intelligimus, remissionem peccatorum non nisi in ecclesia dari, apud haereticos autem, ubi ecclesia non sit, non posse peccata dimitti." (Cf. Kattenbusch, II. p. 372 seq.)

But in the writings of Tertullian we have definite testimony not only to the existence of a symbol, but also to its text. And while its form as reproduced by Tertullian is not identical at every point with the form given by Rufinus and Marcellus it is evidently in large part the same symbol as theirs. The following passages make this sufficiently clear. *De Praescriptione Haereticorum*, 13: "Regula est autem fidei, ut jam hinc quid defendamus profiteamur, illa scilicet qua creditur unum omnino deum esse, nec alium praeter mundi conditorem," etc. (for the remainder of the passage, see p. 86); ibid., 36: "Si autem Italiae adjaces, habes Romam, unde nobis quoque auctoritas praesto est . . . Videamus quid didicerit, quid docuerit, cum Africanis quoque ecclesiis contesserarit. Unum deum dominum novit," etc. (for the remainder of the passage, see p. 87); *De Virginibus Velandis*, 1: "Regula quidem fidei una omnino est, sola immobilis et irreformabilis, credendi scilicet in unicum deum omnipotentem," etc. (for the remainder of the passage, see p. 85); *Adversus Praxeam*, 2: "Nos vero et semper et nunc magis, ut instructiores per paracletum, deductorem scilicet omnis veritatis, unicum quidem deum credimus," etc. (for the remainder of the passage, see p. 86); *De Corona*, 3: "Dehinc ter mergitamur amplius aliquid respondentes quam Dominus in evangelio determinavit;" *De Praescriptione Haereticorum*, 14: "Ceterum manente forma ejus in suo ordine quantumlibet quaeras et tractes et omnem libidinem curiositatis effundas." Compare also *De Praescriptione Haereticorum*, 12, 21, and *Adv. Prax.*, 3.

As there is general agreement among scholars that Tertullian knew the Old Roman Symbol, it is not necessary to discuss the matter more fully here, but simply to refer to Kattenbusch, II. p. 53 seq.

The question whether Irenæus knew the Old Roman Symbol is more difficult. At the same time, there are good reasons for thinking that he did. That he knew and used, or at any rate felt the influence of, some definite symbol seems evident from the following considerations:[1]

1. He refers frequently to a *regula veritatis* (I. 22:1; III. 11:1), or *traditio* (III. 3:3; III. 4:

[1] I have used Harvey's edition of the works of Irenæus, but for the convenience of the reader I have given the references according to the chapter divisions of Massuet (the Benedictine edition) and Stieren, which are followed by the English translation of Irenæus in the "Ante-Nicene Fathers" (published by the Christian Literature Company). As these divisions are indicated by Harvey in the margin, the passages referred to can be found, whichever edition is in the hands of the reader.

2; V. 20:1), or *fides* (I. 10:1; III. 4:2), whose content he then proceeds to give in a more or less definite and stereotyped form. The statements differ considerably in the various passages, but in every case there is a reference to One God Almighty (sometimes One God the Father Almighty) and in three places, where Christ is referred to at some length, there is practical identity, so far at least as substance goes. This is particularly noticeable in I. 10:1 and III. 4:2, the most definite of all the formulations, where there are elaborate references to Christ, which agree closely, and where in both cases Irenæus passes immediately from the birth to the passion. There are, moreover, certain phrases which recur in some of the passages mentioned as well as in others where Irenæus states his faith.

2. Irenæus' formulations have at least in three cases the threefold structure, which suggests a baptismal symbol. Thus in I. 10:1; IV. 33:7; V. 20:1.

3. We have the statement in I. 9:4 that the *regula veritatis* (κανὼν τῆς ἀληθείας) was received "through baptism," and this, taken in connection with I. 10:1, which immediately follows, points to a definite, fixed formula.

But if Irenæus knew any creed it is evident that it was not authoritative in such a sense that he felt obliged to follow it literally. It seems to have influenced him and to have reflected itself in his writings only as any convenient and familiar summary of the common faith of the church might have done. Can we then determine its content and form?

More or less definite formulations occur in I. 10: 1; I. 22: 1; III. 1: 2; III. 3: 3; III. 4: 2; III. 11: 1; III. 16: 6; IV. 33: 7; V. 20: 1. All of them begin with a declaration of faith in God, which is followed by more or less elaborate references to Christ, and in I. 10: 1; III. 4: 2; IV. 33: 7; V. 20: 1, to the Holy Spirit as well. In the light of these passages we may reconstruct tentatively as follows:

1. Εἰς ἕνα θεὸν πατέρα παντοκράτορα.

This entire article is found only in I. 10: 1, the most elaborate statement of the creed. Εἰς ἕνα θεὸν (in unum deum) is found in all the formulations; πατέρα (patrem) in I. 10: 1; III. 16: 6; V. 20: 1; παντοκράτορα (omnipotentem) in I. 10: 1; I. 22: 1; III. 3: 3; III. 11: 1; IV. 33: 7.

Various additions relating to the creation appear in many passages: thus *qui fecit coelum et terram et mare et omnia quae in eis sunt*, I. 10: 1; *qui omnia condidit per verbum suum, et aptavit, et fecit ex eo, quod non erat*, etc., I. 15; *qui per verbum suum omnia fecit, et visibilia et invisibilia*, III. 11: 7; *factorem coeli et terrae, plasmatorem hominis, qui induxerit cataclysmum*, etc., III. 3 : 3 ; *fabricatorem coeli et terrae, et omnium quae in eis sunt*, III. 4 : 2; *ex quo omnia* IV. 33 : 7. The wide variations at this point, when compared with the stereotyped phrase which precedes, suggest that we have here additions of Irenæus' own, which are just what we should expect over against the Gnostics whom he was endeavoring to refute.

2. Εἰς [ἕνα] Χριστὸν Ἰησοῦν, τὸν υἱὸν τοῦ θεοῦ, [κύριον ἡμῶν].

The article appears in this form, but without κύριον ἡμῶν, in I. 10 : 1. Ἕνα before Χριστόν is found also in III. 1 : 2, and III. 16 : 6, but is wanting in III. 4 : 2, IV. 33 : 7 and V. 20 : 1. Its presence in the creed is doubtful, for its occurrence in III. 16 : 6 is clearly due to Irenæus' argument, and it may well have been added in the other two passages under the same influence.

Κύριον ἡμῶν is found in III. 16 : 6 and IV. 33 : 7; and though not in the formulated statement in I. 10 : 1, it is twice joined with Χριστὸν Ἰησοῦν farther on in the same passage. It is therefore possible that it stood in the creed.

3. τὸν γεννηθέντα ἐκ [Μαρίας τῆς] παρθένου.

The substance of this article, though not in these exact words, appears in I. 10 : 1 (τὴν ἐκ παρθένου γέννησιν, — the grammatical construction demanding the noun instead of the participle); III. 4 : 2 (*ex virgine generationem*) ; and also, not as a part of a formulated creed, in III. 16 : 5 (*qui ex Maria natus est*) and IV. 9 : 2 (*qui ex Maria*). It is significant that no reference is made in any of these passages to the agency of the Holy Spirit in the birth of Jesus, though Irenæus accepted the accounts in Matthew and Luke, as is evident, for instance, from III. 21 : 4.

4. Τὸν παθόντα ἐπὶ Ποντίου Πιλάτου.

The passion is mentioned in I. 10 : 1 (καὶ τὸ πάθος), in III. 4 : 2 (*passus sub Pontio Pilato*), and in III. 16 : 6 (*qui et passus est pro nobis*), the only passages in the list of creedal statements given above, in which details of Christ's historic career are mentioned. In all these cases the reference to the passion follows immediately the reference to the birth (in III. 16 : 6 to the incarnation), and the same is true of III. 16 : 5 and IV. 9 : 2, where the passion is also mentioned (*qui et passus est*). It is worthy of notice that in III. 18 : 3, after quoting 1 Cor. XV. 3, 4, Irenæus, in repeating the substance of what Paul has said, substitutes *passus est* for *mortuus est*, referring to the passion instead of the death.

*Sub Pontio Pilato* is found with *passus* in III. 4 : 2, but not in I. 10 : 1. Its occurrence in the former passage suggests that it had a place in the creed, for there was no particular reason otherwise for Irenæus to mention it. The full name is found nowhere in the New Testament either with *passus* or *crucifixus*, but in referring to Christ, Irenæus adds "crucified under Pontius Pilate" in II. 32: 4 and V. 12: 5, and "suffered under Pontius Pilate" in III. 12: 9. It is thus quite probable that it formed a part of the creed with which Irenæus was acquainted, and was omitted in I. 10: 1 because of its unimportance.

5. Καὶ ἀναστάντα ἐκ νεκρῶν.

The resurrection is mentioned immediately after the passion in I. 10: 1 (καὶ τὴν ἔγερσιν ἐκ νεκρῶν: *resurrectionem a mortuis*), in III. 4: 2 (*et resurgens*), and in III. 16: 6 (*et surrexit propter nos*). III. 16: 5 may also be referred to, where we read *et eundem hunc passum resurrexisse*. In III. 18: 3 after quoting I. Cor. XV. 3, 4, Irenæus continues, "It is clear then that Paul knew no other Christ but him who suffered (παθόντα instead of Paul's ἀπέθανεν) and was buried and rose again (ἀναστάντα instead of Paul's ἐγήγερται), and was born, whom also he calls man." The use of ἀναστάντα here instead of ἐγήγερται is worthy of notice. In both cases the old Latin version of Irenæus has *resurrexit*. In II. 32: 3, where there is no sign of a formulated creed, we read *Dominus surrexit a mortuis in tertia die . . . . et discipulis se manifestavit, et videntibus eis receptus est in coelum.*

There can be no doubt that Christ's resurrection had a place in Irenæus' creed, but the exact form of the article is uncertain. Ἀναστάντα is suggested by III. 18 : 3, and ἐκ νεκρῶν by I. 10 : 1 and II. 32 : 3.

6. Ἀναλημφθέντα εἰς τοὺς οὐρανούς.

The ascension is mentioned only in I. 10 : 1 (καὶ τὴν ἔνσαρκον εἰς τοὺς οὐρανοὺς ἀνάληψιν : *et in carne in coelos ascensionem*), III. 4 : 2 (*et in claritate receptus*), and II. 32 : 3 (*receptus est in coelum*); but the reference to it in these passages is sufficient evidence of its occurrence in the creed. The use of ἀνάληψιν in I. 10 : 1 and of the passive participle *receptus* in the two other passages points to the passive participle ἀναλημφθέντα instead of the active ἀναβάντα.

7. Ἐν τῇ δόξῃ τοῦ Πατρὸς ἐρχόμενον ἀναστῆσαι καὶ κρῖναι πάντας ἀνθρώπους.

That Irenæus' creed contained a reference to the second coming of Christ cannot be doubted, but the form of the article is very uncertain. In I. 10 : 1 we have the elaborate passage : "et de coelis in gloria Patris adventum ejus (ἐν τῇ δόξῃ τοῦ Πατρὸς παρουσίαν αὐτοῦ), ad recapitulanda universa, et resuscitandam omnem carnem humani generis (ἀναστῆσαι πᾶσαν σάρκα πάσης ἀνθρωπότητος), ut Christo Jesu domino nostro, et deo, et salvatori, et regi, secundum placitum Patris invisibilis omne genu curvet coelestium, et terrestrium, et infernorum, et omnis lingua confiteatur ei, et judicium justum in omnibus faciat : spiritalia quidem nequitiae, et angelos transgressos, atque apostatas factos, et impios, et injustos, et iniquos, et blasphemos homines in aeternum ignem mittat: justis autem et aequis, et praecepta ejus servantibus, et in dilectione ejus perseverantibus, quibusdam quidem ab initio, quibusdam autem ex poenitentia, vitam donans incorruptelam loco muneris conferat, et claritatem aeternam circumdet;" in III. 4 : 2 : "in gloria venturus salvator eorum qui salvantur, et judex eorum qui judicantur, et mittens in ignem aeternum transfiguratores veritatis, et contemtores Patris sui et adventus ejus;" in III. 16 : 6 : "et rursus venturus est in gloria Patris, ad resuscitandam universam carnem, et ad ostensionem salutis, et regulam justi judicii ostendere omnibus qui sub ipso facti sunt;" and in V. 20 : 1 : "et eundem exspectantibus adventum domini, et eandem salutem totius hominis, id est animae et corporis, sustinentibus."

That Irenæus' creed contained a reference to the resurrection of the flesh is rendered practically certain by I. 10 : 1 and III. 16 : 6, where it is mentioned as one of the purposes of the return of Christ (I. 10 : 1 : *adventum ejus ad recapitulanda universa, et resuscitandam omnem carnem humani generis;* III. 16 : 6 : *et rursus venturus est in gloria Patris, ad resuscitandam universam carnem*), and also by V. 20: 1, where it is mentioned separately, but immediately after a reference to Christ's coming (*et eundem exspectantibus adventum domini, et eandem salutem totius hominis, id est animae et corporis, sustinentibus*). In III. 4 : 2, the only other passage where the return of Christ is mentioned, there is a reference only to salvation, not specifically to the resurrection. Though the article without doubt had a place in the creed used by Irenæus, it is quite impossible to determine from his writings its form or its position in the creed.

8. Εἰς πνεῦμα ἅγιον.

That the Holy Spirit had a place in Irenæus' creed is clear from I. 10 : 1 (εἰς πνεῦμα ἅγιον), IV. 33 : 7 (εἰς τὸ πνεῦμα τοῦ θεοῦ), and V. 20 : 1 (*et eandem donationem Spiritus scientibus*). That he failed to mention the Spirit in the many other passages which we have been dealing with was due doubtless to the fact that the heretics whom he was combating raised no difficulties in connection with the Spirit.

Having thus tentatively reconstructed the creed used by Irenæus, let us ask what is its relation to the Old Roman Symbol known to Rufinus and Marcellus.

The creed of Irenæus agrees with R [1] in mentioning God Father almighty; Christ Jesus his son; the birth from a virgin; the passion (in R the crucifixion) immediately after the birth; the resurrection of Christ; the ascension; the return of Christ to judge; the resurrection of the flesh; the

[1] I. e., the Old Roman Symbol.

Holy Spirit. It omits altogether the articles on the session at the right hand of the Father, on the church and on the forgiveness of sins. It omits also μονογενῆ in article 2; ἐκ πνεύματος ἁγίου in article 3; σταυρωθέντα καὶ ταφέντα in article 4 (παθόντα occurring instead); and ἐν τρίτῃ ἡμέρᾳ in article 5.

It has no articles which are not found in R, but in article 1 it adds ἕνα before θεόν; in article 4 it has παθόντα (instead of σταυρωθέντα καὶ ταφέντα); in article 6 ἀναλημφθέντα instead of ἀναβάντα; and article 7, on the return of Christ, is more elaborate than in R and quite different in form.

This comparison shows clearly that the creed of Irenæus and the Old Roman Symbol cannot be independent of each other. The resemblances are so close and the differences so few that we must assume that Irenæus knew the Old Roman Symbol either in the form known to Rufinus, or, as is more probable, in a briefer and somewhat variant form. Whether he knew it as a creed in use in the church of Rome is less certain, but his references to Rome in III. 3: 2 and 3 make it very likely that he did. At any rate, we have in Irenæus a witness to the existence of the creed we know as the Old Roman Symbol in nearly if not quite its present form as early as the year 175. Upon Irenæus' relation to R, see also Kattenbusch, II. p. 25 seq.

Let us push our inquiry still further back and ask whether the creed was known to Marcion and his Gnostic contemporaries.

Kattenbusch maintains that R was already in use in Rome as a *Regula Fidei* when Marcion came thither, and that he gave in his adherence to it when he joined the Catholic Church there (cf. II. p. 86 seq., 322 seq.). The same view is taken by Zahn (p. 31 seq.). The grounds upon which this opinion is based seem to me to need much more careful investigation than they have yet received. Both Zahn and Kattenbusch make altogether too easy work of the matter. The only sources we have which throw any light upon the question at issue are the writings of Tertullian, particularly his *Adversus Marcionem, De Carne Christi,* and *De Praescriptione Haereticorum.*

According to Kattenbusch (II. p. 86), who goes into the matter more carefully than Zahn, Tertullian's repeated references to an epistle in which Marcion had testified that his faith agreed with the faith of the church of Rome, and his declaration that Marcion after being excluded from the church had been again admitted to the *confessio paenitentiae,* show that Marcion knew R, and continued to accept it in his own way, even after his excommunication. And this conclusion is confirmed, according to Kattenbusch, by the fact that Marcion's disciples maintained "Marcionem non tam innovasse regulam separatione legis et evangelii, quam retro adulteratam recurasse" (*Adv. Marc.*, I. 20), where the context shows that the word *regula* was understood by Marcion in the same sense as by Tertullian, that is as referring to R.

Let us first examine Marcion's letter, to which Tertullian appeals in support of his claim that Marcion originally agreed with the faith of the Roman church. Tertullian is our only witness to the existence of such a letter, and he mentions it in only three passages — *Adv. Marc.*, I. 1 : " Non negabunt discipuli ejus primam illius fidem nobiscum fuisse, ipsius litteris testibus ; " *De Carne Christi*, 2 : " Excidisti, rescindendo quod retro credidisti, sicut et ipse confiteris in quadam epistula et tui non negant et nostri probant ; " *Adv. Marc.*, IV. 4 : " Quid nunc, si negaverint Marcionitae primam apud nos fidem ejus adversus epistulam quoque ipsius? Quid si nec epistulam agnoverint ? "

It seems clear from the very general nature of Tertullian's references to the letter in these passages and from the fact that he nowhere quotes directly from it, either that he had never seen the letter, or that it was of so general a character as not to lend itself to quotation. If Tertullian had not himself seen it, the authenticity of the letter must be recognized to be at best very doubtful, and his words in *Adv. Marc.*, IV. 4 : " Quid nunc si nec epistulam agnoverint," go to confirm the doubt. Kattenbusch and Zahn have strangely failed to call attention to this circumstance and have treated the letter as of unquestioned authenticity.

But, assuming that Tertullian had actually seen the letter and that it was authentic, what must have been its character ? Had it contained a definite *regula* or creed, either R or one of Marcion's own, or had it definitely stated Marcion's belief on any important points in which he afterward departed from the faith of the church, Tertullian would certainly have quoted from it in his effort to show that Marcion had once held the faith of the Roman church. And had it contained the explicit statement that Marcion accepted R, Tertullian would have said so in clearer terms than he uses. The words : " primam illius fidem nobiscum fuisse; " " primam apud nos fidem ejus; " " excidisti, rescindendo quod retro credidisti " are quite too indefinito to establish Marcion's acceptance of R, or any other particular creed. Moreover if Marcion had explicitly asserted his acceptance of R, or if he had distinctly said that he once agreed with the faith of the Roman church, or of the church at large, his followers could not have denied that he did, as some of them seem to have done even while not denying the authenticity of the letter (cf. *Adv. Marc.*, IV. 4).

In the light of these considerations it would seem that the letter if authentic contained at most only a general reference to the fact that Marcion's faith had undergone a change since the early days of his Christian life, a reference which would of course justify his opponents in claiming that he had once agreed completely with the faith of the church and had afterward departed from it, while it would make it possible for his disciples to deny that he had ever accepted that faith. It is clear then that we are not justified in using the letter as a proof that Marcion ever knew and accepted R.[1]

Another proof that Marcion knew and accepted R is found by Kattenbusch in *De Praescriptione Haereticorum*, 30, where it is said that Marcion and Valentinus were at first believers in the doctrine of the Catholic church (*in catholicae primo doctrinam credidisse*), until on account of their ever restless curiosity, with which they infected the brethren, they were more than once expelled from the church, and that afterward Marcion confessed repentance and agreed to the condition imposed

---

[1] If the letter was of the character indicated, it is plain that it cannot have been addressed to the Roman church at the time Marcion applied for membership with the purpose of allaying suspicion and so making it possible for the church to accept him, as Kattenbusch holds. So that Kattenbusch's description of it as a letter " worin Marcion dieser Gemeinde [i. e., the church of Rome] *ihre* fides als *seine* fides bezeugt habe" must be pronounced altogether inaccurate. And the same may be said of Zahn's reference to the letter, *Das Apostolische Symbolum*, p. 31.

upon him, that he should be received back if he restored to the church those whom he had led astray ("Postmodum Marcion paenitentiam confessus cum condicioni datae sibi occurrit, ita pacem recepturus, si ceteros quos perditioni erudisset ecclesiae restitueret, morte praeventus est"). I am quite unable to find any hint of a creed or symbol in this passage and I am at a loss to understand how Kattenbusch can regard it as supporting his claim that Marcion knew and accepted R. He says "Tertullian redet wiederholt von dem Briefe, worin Marcion dieser Gemeinde *ihre* fides als *seine* fides bezeugt habe, sowie davon, dass er, der wegen seiner inquieta curiositas 'dauernd' ausgeschlossen worden sei, zuletzt doch noch wieder zur 'confessio paenitentiae' zugelassen wäre. Darin liegt indirekt, dass er am Symbol in seiner Weise *dauernd* festgehalten hat." These words seem to show that he assumes that the phrase *paenitentiam confessus* points to the acceptance of R by Marcion, but the assumption is entirely gratuitous.

Kattenbusch refers again in support of his contention that Marcion knew and accepted R, to *Adv. Marc.*, I. 20, where Tertullian says "Aiunt enim Marcionem non tam innovasse regulam separatione legis et evangelii quam retro adulteratam recurasse." Kattenbusch takes *regula* in this passage as referring to R, but *regula* is a word of varying connotation in Tertullian, and the context alone can determine its meaning in any particular passage. A brief examination of Tertullian's use of the word will make this plain.

1. *Regula* is used of a definite creed or formula in *Adv. Prax.*, 2, 9; *regula fidei* in *Adv. Prax.*, 3; *De Praescriptione*, 12, 13; *De Virg. Vel.*, 1; *De Monogamia*, 2; *regula fidei aut spei* in *De Jejunio*, 1, where the addition of *spei* makes it a little doubtful whether a definite creed is meant.

2. *Regula* is used in other senses in the following passages: *Adv. Marc.*, I. 1, where it refers to Marcion's teaching in general, for Tertullian says he will report Marcion's *regula,* and what he actually does is to enter into a general discussion of his system and of his Biblical criticism. The same general use of the word occurs in *Adv. Marc.*, IV. 17, where Marcion's disciples are said to have deserted the *regula* of their master in abandoning his view of the judgment because of its inconsistencies. There is no hint of a creed here, but only of Marcion's teaching in regard to the judgment and God's relation to it contained in his Antitheses. In *Adv. Marc.*, I. 5, *regula* signifies a rule or law of logic. In *Adv. Marc.*, I. 22, it means a fixed principle or method of examining God's goodness. In *Adv. Marc.*, IV. 5, it refers to the law according to which the Galatians were corrected by Paul. In the same chapter again it

signifies the content or the teaching of the three other gospels with which the Gospel of Luke agrees. In *Adv. Marc.*, IV. 2, it is said that Paul, when he went up to Jerusalem to consult the apostles about his gospel "that he might not run in vain," agreed with them touching the *regula fidei*, where the word evidently refers, not to any definite creed or symbol, but to the gospel preached by both them and him. The point of the whole passage is that Tertullian finds the legitimation of Paul's gospel in the approval given to it by the older apostles, and so demands that the Gospel of Luke, which was written by a disciple of Paul, shall be legitimatized by its agreement with the other gospels. In *Adv. Marc.*, III. 17, occurs the phrase *regula scripturarum*, which refers not to a creed but to the principle of scripture interpretation. In *Apol.*, 46, the phrase *regula disciplinæ* is used of the Christian law of morality or conduct.

3. The meaning of the word *regula* is doubtful in the following passages: *De Praescriptione Haereticorum*, 3, where falling away from the *regula* is spoken of, and where it is uncertain whether the orthodox creed is meant or the Christian faith or religion in a more general sense; *De Praescriptione*, 42, where heretics are accused of departing from their own *regulae*, which may or may not be formal statements of belief; *De Praescriptione*, 44, where Christ is represented as saying "semel

evangelium et ejusdem regulae doctrinam apostolis meis delegaveram; libuit mihi postea aliqua inde mutare," and where it is doubtful whether *ejusdem regulae* means a creed or the general law of faith and conduct given by Christ. Again in *Adv. Marc.*, I. 21, and III. 1, it is uncertain whether Tertullian refers to a definite symbol, or simply to the unformulated belief of the church.

In the light of all these passages it is clear that the occurrence of the word *regula* in *Adv. Marc.*, I. 20, does not of itself prove that Tertullian is there referring to R or to any other definite creed. And an examination of the context makes it evident that he is thinking not of a creed but rather of the canon of scripture. In the passage immediately preceding he speaks of Marcion's separation of law and gospel which is set forth in his Antitheses, where the contradictions between the old and the new *instrumenti* are exhibited. And he then goes on, after using the words quoted above ("Aiunt enim Marcionem non tam innovasse regulam separatione legis et evangelii quam retro adulteratam recurasse"), to speak of the controversy between Peter and Paul touching circumcision and the observance of the law, and to show that the abrogation of the Jewish ceremonial law and the substitution of a new spiritual covenant had been prophesied in the Old Testament. In the entire section there is no hint of a creed or symbol of any kind, and to interpret *regula* as referring to such a creed or symbol is to do violence to the context.

Finally Kattenbusch, following Zahn, appeals to *De Carne Christi*, 2, in proof of his claim that Marcion knew and accepted R. The passage, a part of which was quoted above in connection with the discussion of Marcion's letter, runs as follows: "His, opinor, consiliis tot originalia instrumenta Christi delere, Marcion, ausus es, ne caro ejus probaretur. Ex quo, oro te? Exhibe auctoritatem. Si propheta es, prænuntia aliquid: si apostolus, praedica publice: si apostolicus, cum apostolis senti: si tantum christianus es, crede quod traditum est: si nihil istorum es, merito dixerim, morere. Nam et mortuus es, qui non es christianus, non credendo quod creditum christianos facit, et eo magis mortuus es quo magis non es christianus, qui cum fuisses, excidisti, rescindendo quod retro credidisti, sicut et ipse confiteris in quadam epistula et tui non negant et nostri probant. Igitur rescindens quod credidisti jam non credens rescidisti, non tamen quia credere desisti, recte rescidisti, atquin rescindendo quod credidisti probas ante quam rescinderes aliter fuisse. Quod credidisti aliter, illud ita erat traditum. Porro quod traditum erat, id erat verum, ut ab eis traditum quorum fuit tradere. Ergo quod erat traditum rescindens quod erat verum rescidisti. Nullo jure fecisti. Sed plenius ejusmodi præscriptionibus adversus omnes haereses alibi jam usi sumus. Post quas nunc ex abundanti retractamus, desiderantes rationem qua non putaveris natum esse Christum." When the passage is read in its entirety and in connection with the context it is perfectly clear that Tertullian is referring not to Marcion's rejection of a creed or symbol which he had once accepted, but to his blotting out of the record of Christ's birth contained in the gospels. The whole discussion concerns the reality of Christ's nativity, and Tertullian goes over the events attending Christ's birth and infancy as recounted in the gospels — the annunciation, the conception, the imperial taxing, the crowded inn, the stable, the swaddling clothes, the song of the angels, the shepherds, the wise men, the circumcision, the presentation in the temple — and then asks Marcion by what authority he has blotted out the record of all these things (*originalia instrumenta Christi delere*).[1]

---

[1] One needs only to read the whole chapter to see how wide of the mark is the following note of Zahn (*Das apostolische Symbolum*, p. 31): " Entscheidend scheinen mir besonders folgende Ausdrücke zu sein (*De Carne Christi*, 2): Mortuus es, qui non es Christianus, non credendo quod creditum (al. traditum) Christianos facit. — Quod credidisti aliter, illud ita erat traditum. Unaufhörlich werden dort die Worte credidisti und traditum wiederholt." If the words credidisti and traditum stood by themselves one might easily suppose they referred to a creed or symbol, but such a reference is seen to be impossible when the context is examined.

Thus all the passages urged by Kattenbusch in support of the claim that Marcion knew and accepted R, when carefully examined, are seen not to bear the interpretation which he puts upon them. There is no evidence in them nor is there evidence anywhere that Marcion knew and accepted R. And the lack of such evidence makes strongly against the supposition that he did, for it is just the kind of fact which we should have expected Marcion's opponents to make good use of in their controversy with him.

And not simply is there no evidence that Marcion knew and accepted R, there is no evidence that he had any definite creed or symbol. We have explicit testimony to the existence of his scripture canon and of his Antitheses but of no other documents handed down by him to his followers, and certainly had there been any such we should have heard of them.

Concerning the relation of Valentinus and other early Gnostics to R we have even less information than for Marcion. The statements that Valentinus originally accepted the doctrine of the Catholic Church (Tertullian, *De Praescriptione Haereticorum*, 30), and that the Valentinians were accustomed to declare that they held the same faith as the church at large (Irenæus, III. 15 : 2 ; Tertullian, *Adv. Val.*, 1), are of the most general character and may or may not point to the acceptance of the same creed.

That the Valentinians had creeds or symbols of their own is quite possible (cf. Tertullian, *Adv. Val.*, 4 ; *De Praescriptione*, 42, 44, which may or may not refer to definite creeds or symbols), but of their relation to R we know nothing. It is possible that Apelles, the famous Marcionite, had a creed framed after the pattern of R, as maintained by Harnack (see his *De Apellis Gnosi Monarchica*, p. 31 seq., and Hahn, p. 377), but he was a contemporary of Irenæus and his testimony does not carry us back beyond the last quarter of the second century.

Let us turn next to Justin Martyr and the other apologists of the day.

Justin nowhere in his extant works testifies to the existence of any creed or symbol ; but his writings contain many stereotyped phrases and collocations of words which suggest at first sight an acquaintance with R or with some symbol more or less closely akin to it.

It is not necessary to repeat the evidence which is given in detail by Bornemann in an elaborate article in the *Zeitschrift für Kirchengeschichte*, 1879, p. 1-27, and also by Kattenbusch, II. p. 286, 293 seq. I may simply call attention to some of the most important points.

The first article of R — θεὸν πατέρα παντοκράτορα — is not found in Justin, but the word παντοκράτωρ occurs six times (*Dial.*, 16, 38, 83, 96, 139, 142), five times with θεός, and once (*Dial.* 139) with πατήρ. The phrase θεὸς παντοκράτωρ is common in the LXX and in the Johannine Apocalypse, but πατὴρ παντοκράτωρ occurs nowhere before Justin. God is commonly called by Justin "Father of the universe," "God and Father of the Universe" or "of all," "Father and Maker of all things," "Maker of Heaven and Earth," "Father of Christ," etc.

The particulars of the third section of R (Holy Spirit, Holy Church, Forgiveness of sins, Resurrection of flesh) are nowhere associated by Justin. He speaks often of the Spirit, commonly as "the prophetic Spirit," or "Holy Spirit of Prophecy," never as πνεῦμα ἅγιον without article or qualifying phrase as in R. He also refers twice to the church (*Dial.* 63, 134), a few times to the forgiveness of sins (ἄφεσις ἁμαρτιῶν), and still oftener to the resurrection, commonly as a resurrection of bodies, only once as a resurrection of flesh (σαρκὸς ἀνάστασις, *Dial.*, 80). There is no sign in any of these cases of the influence of R, or of any other symbol.

In speaking of Christ, Justin refers over and over again to the virgin birth (διὰ παρθένου), but does not mention the Spirit in connection with it. Christ's teaching and wonderful works, his crucifixion, suffering, death, burial, resurrection, ascension, session, and second coming are also spoken

## DATE OF THE OLD ROMAN SYMBOL

of, some of them more, some less frequently. There are about a dozen passages in which various events in Christ's career are mentioned together, more or less after the fashion of R. Thus the birth, works, crucifixion, death, resurrection, ascension (*Apol.*, I. 31); virgin birth, crucifixion, death, resurrection, ascension (*Apol.*, I. 46); incarnation through the Virgin, suffering, crucifixion, death, resurrection, ascension (*Dial.*, 89); birth, death, resurrection (*Apol.*, I. 63); birth, suffering, ascension (*Dial.*, 126); birth, crucifixion (*Apol.*, I. 13); crucifixion, death, resurrection, ascension (*Apol.*, I. 21, 42); crucifixion, death, resurrection (*Dial.*, 65); crucifixion, resurrection, ascension (*Apol.*, I. 50); crucifixion, resurrection, ascension, judgment (*Dial.*, 132); crucifixion, suffering, lordship (*Dial.*, 76); burial, resurrection, judgment (*Dial.*, 118).

There is no verbal agreement between these various passages or between any of them and R, and they are in no case associated with references to God and the Holy Spirit so as to suggest that they are a part of a creed as in R. The most one can say is that Justin has in mind certain events in connection with Christ, at least some of which he mentions frequently and in more or less stereotyped form. But such stereotyping as we find may easily have preceded the formation of R. The events mentioned by Justin are just the ones which he might have been expected to emphasize, whether or not they had been previously connected in a formula; and the use of prophecy would naturally lead to the collocation of such events in order to make the appeal to prophecy more telling.

But the repeated use of the phrase "Crucified under Pontius Pilate" demands still further explanation. The phrase is a standing one with Justin and is used over and over again when there is no reason in the context for its introduction, and when it can be explained only as a familiar and stereotyped phrase which suggested itself naturally at the mention of Christ's name. Thus, for instance, in connection with the formula of baptism in *Apol.*, I. 61, Justin says: "Into the name of the father of the universe and Lord God, and of Jesus Christ who was crucified under Pontius Pilate, and of the Holy Spirit who through the prophets foretold all things concerning Jesus."

The crucifixion is referred to seventy-six times in Justin's writings and in the majority of cases in connection with the exorcism of demons. Thus, for instance, in *Apol.*, II. 6, it is said: "For many of our people — that is the Christians — have healed and are now healing numberless demoniacs throughout the world and in your own city, exorcising them in the name of Jesus Christ, who was crucified under Pontius Pilate, overcoming and driving out the devils who possessed them though they could not be cured by all the other exorcists and users of drugs and incantations;" and again in *Dial.*, 30: "For we call him helper and redeemer, the power of whose name even the demons tremble at; and to-day when they are exorcised in the name of Jesus Christ, who was crucified under Pontius Pilate, Governor of Judea, they obey." (Cf. also *Dial.*, 49, 85). These and other similar passages suggest that the words "Jesus Christ, who was crucified under Pontius Pilate" constituted a regular formula of exorcism which was so familiar to Justin that it naturally came into his mind whenever he mentioned Christ's name. And so in *Apol.*, I. 61, in defining more particularly the three persons into whose names the convert was baptized, he naturally used the stereotyped phrase "crucified under Pontius Pilate" in speaking of Christ, as he used familiar and current phrases in speaking of God and of the Holy Spirit.

In the article mentioned above Bornemann maintains that Justin had a creed similar to, though not identical with R, and he attempts to reconstruct it in detail upon the basis of Justin's use of stereotyped phrases such as have been referred to. But the evidence is utterly inadequate to establish Bornemann's conclusion. If Justin testified distinctly to the existence of a creed in his day, or if we knew on other grounds that a creed was in general use or in use at Rome when he was writing we might perhaps see in some passages quotations from or echoes of such a creed, but taken by themselves they prove nothing beyond the natural and common tendency to emphasize certain events in Christ's life, or to use certain more or less stereotyped phrases in speaking of Christian facts and truths. Kattenbusch recognizes the error in Bornemann's method and rejects altogether his reconstruction of Justin's creed. But he maintains that Justin knew R, and he finds many reminiscences of it in his writings. At the same time he admits if we were not already acquainted with R we could not attribute to Justin a knowledge of any symbol, and if we did not know that R was in use in Rome in Justin's time we could not gather sufficient evidence from his writings to prove it. It is only because we know that R was in use in Rome when Marcion came thither that we are justified, according to Kattenbusch, in finding echoes of it in Justin's writings. But we have already seen that there is absolutely no evidence that Marcion knew or used R, and so the presumption with which Kattenbusch comes to the study of Justin does not exist for us; and that being the case we must recognize that there is no ground for the assertion that Justin knew and used R or any other creed or symbol.

But it seems to me we may go further than this and say that there is on the contrary good evidence that he did not know R or any similar symbol. In *Apol.*, I. 61, 65–67, he gives an elaborate account of Christian worship, including a detailed description of the rite of baptism. He opens his account with the words : " I will also relate the manner in which we dedicated ourselves to God when we had been made new through Christ; lest if we omit this we seem to do wrong in the explanation we are making." (Compare chapter 3, where he says : " Every sober-minded person will declare that this is a fair and just demand, that those accused render an unexceptional account of their own life and doctrine ; " and a little farther on " It is our business, therefore, to afford to all an opportunity of inspecting our life and teachings.") And he then continues : " As many as are persuaded and believe that what we teach and say is true, and undertake to be able to live accordingly, are instructed to pray and to ask from God, with fasting, the remission of their past sins, we praying and fasting with them. Then they are brought by us where there is water, and are regenerated in the same manner in which we were ourselves regenerated. For in the name of the Father of the universe and Lord God, and of our Saviour Jesus Christ, and of the Holy Spirit, they then receive the washing with water."

There is no mention of a creed or symbol anywhere in the passage. It might be thought that a creed is referred to in the words, "As many as are persuaded and believe that what we teach and say is true," but the reference may be simply to Christian faith in general, and that it cannot refer specifically to R or to any similar symbol is proved by what follows: "and undertake to be able to live accordingly." Evidently ethical instruction is chiefly in mind and we are reminded at once of the *Didache* with its prebaptismal moral instruction. The omission of all reference to a creed in Justin's description of Christian baptism seems to me to prove conclusively that no such creed as R was current in Rome at the time he wrote, for R is evidently based upon the baptismal formula, and was from the beginning without question a baptismal symbol.

On Justin's relation to R see also Harnack in the *Zeitschrift für Theologie und Kirche*, 1894, p. 147 seq.

The other Greek Apologists of the second century make no reference to R and none of them, with the possible exception of Aristides of Athens and Melito of Sardis, contains any trace of a knowledge of R or of any other creed. So far as Aristides is concerned, Kattenbusch (II. p. 303 seq.) thinks that there may possibly be a reminiscence of R in the following passage: ἐν πνεύματι ἁγίῳ ἀπ' οὐρανοῦ καταβὰς διὰ τὴν σωτηρίαν τῶν ἀνθρώπων. καὶ ἐκ παρθένου ἁγίας γεννηθεὶς, ἀσπόρως τε καὶ ἀφθόρως, σάρκα ἀνέλαβε, καὶ ἀνεφάνη ἀνθρώποις ... καὶ τελέσας τὴν θαυμαστὴν αὐτοῦ οἰκονομίαν, διὰ σταυροῦ θανάτου ἐγεύσατο ... μετὰ δὲ τρεῖς ἡμέρας ἀνεβίω καὶ εἰς οὐρανοὺς ἀνῆλθεν (*Apol.*, 2).

But even granting that the above represents the original text, which is not certain, the most that can be said is that if it could be shown on other grounds that Aristides knew R it might be thought that he had R in mind while he was speaking of virgin birth, crucifixion, resurrection, and ascension; but as there is no other evidence of his acquaintance with R or with any other symbol, the passage quoted is far too general in character to prove anything. There is nothing in the passage which may not be easily explained as a free composition of Aristides, writing under the influence of the common Gospel tradition.

In the case of Melito of Sardis, a contemporary of Irenæus, the evidence of an acquaintance with R is more marked. Melito nowhere refers to R or to any other creed, but in one of the Syriac fragments of his writings, the authenticity of which is not altogether certain, occurs the following passage: " Ipse qui in virgine corporatus est, ipse qui in ligno suspensus est, ipse qui in terra sepultus est, ipse qui e mortuis surrexit et ascendit ad altitudinem cœli et sedet ad dexteram patris."[1] Assuming that this passage is really authentic, the identity of the series of events with the series in R (birth, crucifixion, burial, resurrection, ascension, and session) is very striking, and especially the phrase *ad dexteram patris*, which is found nowhere else in second century literature except in R, in Irenæus, and in Tertullian (see p. 97). It certainly looks as if Melito were acquainted with R, and, as he was a contemporary of Irenæus and the intercourse between Asia Minor and the west was very active, it is quite possible that he was. But in the absence of collateral testimony to the use of R in the east at this time, and in view of the uncertainty touching the authenticity of the fragment in question, and in view also of the fact that the Syriac manuscript containing the fragment dates from the sixth century, when the Nicæno-Constantinopolitan creed with the same series of events (except for the addition of παθόντα) and with the phrase ἐκ δεξιῶν τοῦ πατρός, was current in the east, it will not do to speak with any positiveness.

Upon Melito's relation to R see Kattenbusch, II. p. 229 seq.

There is no hint of a knowledge of R or of any other creed in First and Second Clement and The Shepherd of Hermas, all of which were writ-

[1] Otto: *Corpus Apologetarum Christianorum*, vol. ix., p. 423.

ten in Rome, and the last two probably not far from the middle of the second century. The silence of these three witnesses, especially of the last two, goes to confirm the conclusion already reached that R was not in use in Rome before the middle of that century. Kattenbusch admits that these writers contain no testimony to the existence of R, but he nevertheless pushes its origin back to about 100 (i. e., to a time shortly after the composition of 1 Clement), treating the silence of Hermas and 2 Clement as of no significance. But such a course is possible only to one who maintains, as Kattenbusch does, that we have positive testimony that R was in use in Rome when Marcion came thither. When one recognizes that we have no testimony to that effect, and that Justin Martyr's writings make against rather than for the existence of R in Rome in his day, the silence of Hermas and 2 Clement is full of meaning.

What is true of Hermas and the two Clements is true also of all the other apostolic fathers. Not one of them shows any trace of a knowledge of any kind of a symbol or creed. The silence of the *Didache* is especially significant, for it contains an elaborate account of the rite of baptism, including the pre-baptismal instruction to be given to the candidate, and if that instruction embraced R or any other creed the writer could not have failed to mention it. As it is, the instruction given is wholly moral and practical (cf. *Did.*, I–VI). This may be regarded as conclusive evidence that no symbol or creed was in use at the time when the *Didache* was written (probably the early part of the second century), at any rate in that part of the church to which it belongs, that is, in Syria or Palestine.

A few words should be said about Ignatius, for his epistles contain some passages which have been thought by many scholars (Caspari, Zahn, and others) to indicate his acquaintance with R or with some similar symbol (cf. especially Zahn, *Ignatius von Antiochien*, p. 590 seq.). Ignatius nowhere refers to a symbol or creed. It is true that he sometimes uses the word πίστις in an objective sense (e. g., in *Eph.* 16 and 20), but there is no sign that he had anything more definite in mind than the faith of the church, or the true belief concerning Christ, quite irrespective of its formulation in a creed. In *Magn.*, 13, he exhorts his readers to be "confirmed in the ordinances (δόγματα) of the Lord and of the Apostles," but the context shows that he refers to practical ordinances, which have to do with conduct, not with faith; and the same practical interest leads him to exhort the Magnesians, in chap. 11, to be "fully persuaded concerning the birth, and the passion, and the resurrection, which took place in the time of the governorship of Pontius Pilate."

The only passages that furnish any possible support to the claim that Ignatius had a creed are two containing more or less stereotyped accounts of the career of Christ or references to certain events in that career which suggest such a formulation as we have in the second article of R. Thus in *Trall.*, 9: "Be ye deaf therefore when any man speaketh to you apart from Jesus Christ, who was of the race of David, who was son of Mary (τοῦ ἐκ Μαρίας), who was truly born (ἀληθῶς ἐγεννήθη), and ate and drank, was truly persecuted under Pontius Pilate, was truly crucified and died (ἀληθῶς ἐσταυρώθη καὶ ἀπέθανεν) in the sight of those in heaven and on earth and under the earth, who also was truly raised from the dead (ἀληθῶς ἠγέρθη ἀπὸ νεκρῶν), his Father having raised him, who in like manner will so raise us also who believe in him — his Father will raise us in Christ Jesus, apart from whom we have not true life"; *Smyrn.*, 1: "For I have perceived that ye are established in faith immovable, . . . being fully persuaded concerning our Lord, that he is truly of the seed of David in flesh, son of God in will and power, truly born of a virgin (γεγεννημένον ἀληθῶς ἐκ παρθένου), baptized by John that all righteousness might be fulfilled by him, truly nailed up in flesh for our sakes under Pontius Pilate and Herod the Tetrarch (of which fruit are we; that is of his most blessed passion); that he might set up an ensign unto all the ages through the resurrection, for his saints and faithful people, whether among Jews or Gentiles, in one body of his church."

It is to be noticed that in both these passages Ignatius is opposing docetists who deny the reality of Christ's earthly body, and so he is interested to emphasize its reality in the strongest possible way. This consideration fully accounts for the mention of Jesus' Davidic lineage, his birth, his baptism, his eating and drinking, his passion, crucifixion, death, and resurrection, and no formulated creed is needed to explain such mention. So far as the phraseology goes it varies greatly in the two cases and the slight stereotyping of expression at some points, in these and other passages, is no more than one might expect in a writer who felt it necessary to insist so strenuously and continually upon the reality of Christ's life over against docetism.

It is to be noticed again that the more or less formulated references to the career of Christ which have been mentioned are not connected by Ignatius with articles concerning God or the Holy Spirit; in other words they do not appear as part of a three-membered symbol, as is the case in R, and so their connection with a creed is rendered still more improbable.

Finally the failure of Ignatius to refer explicitly

to a creed in his conflict with the docetists, and especially in *Phil.* 8, where his opponents refuse to accept his account of Christ on the ground that it is not found in the Archives (ἀρχείοις) or Old Testament, seems to me conclusive evidence that he had no creed or symbol. For a fuller discussion of Ignatius see Harnack in the *Expositor*, Dec. 1885, Jan. and March 1886, and Kattenbusch, II. p. 310 seq., both of whom deny that Ignatius had a creed.

It is not necessary to go any further back in our examination of early christian literature. There is not even the remotest trace of R or of any other formulated creed in the writings of the New Testament. So far, then, as the testimony of the extant documents goes, R must have originated in the third quarter of the second century, in the interval between the literary activity of Justin Martyr and that of Irenæus. We shall see later whether the internal evidence to be drawn from R itself confirms or contradicts this conclusion.

## III.

### THE ORIGINAL TEXT OF THE OLD ROMAN SYMBOL.

It is maintained by Harnack and Kattenbusch that the text of R, as we find it testified to by Rufinus in the fourth century, is the original text. The reasons for their opinion do not clearly appear. As a matter of fact, neither of them seems to have made earnest with the question whether the fourth century text of R may not be an enlargement of the earliest form, except in so far as relates to the first article, where they discuss carefully Zahn's contention that it read originally πιστεύω εἰς ἕνα Θεὸν παντοκράτορα. The fact that Rufinus says that the church of Rome had preserved its symbol from the beginning unchanged (*Expositio Symboli*, chap. 3) of course proves nothing, for Rufinus' testimony is of weight at most for only a generation or two. The fact, moreover, that the theological discussions of the third century did not result in a complete transformation of the symbol, or in large additions to it, as happened for instance in the east where the Logos christology found its way into the text, does not prove that no additions were made at any time and under any circumstances. There is indeed no a priori reason why the fourth century text of R may not be an enlargement of the original form. The only way to determine whether it is or not is to examine the testimony of the earliest witnesses to the creed, that is especially of Irenæus and Tertullian.

In trying to discover the text of R as known to them it is to be borne in mind that both of them are very free in their treatment of the creed, and that their testimony to its text is therefore to be used with caution. Tertullian follows the letter of the creed more closely than Irenæus, and declares that the *regula fidei* is *una omnino, sola immobilis et irreformabilis*, but even he reproduces it in different forms at different times, showing that it is its substance, not its form, with which he is chiefly concerned.

The principal passages upon which we have to base a reconstruction of the text of the creed as known to Tertullian are *De Virginibus Velandis*, 1, the most compact and apparently the most exact statement of it; *Adv. Praxeam*, 2, and *De Praescriptione Haereticorum*, 13, which are more elaborate, and *De Praescriptione Haereticorum*, 36, which is only fragmentary. These passages run as follows: *De Virg. Vel.* 1: " Regula quidem fidei una omnino est, sola immobilis et irreformabilis, credendi scilicet in unicum Deum omnipotentem, mundi conditorem, et filium ejus Jesum Christum, natum ex virgine Maria, crucifixum sub Pontio

Pilato, tertia die resuscitatum a mortuis, receptum in coelis, sedentem nunc ad dexteram patris, venturum judicare vivos et mortuos per carnis etiam resurrectionem." *Adv. Prax.*, 2 : " Nos vero et semper et nunc magis, ut instructiores per paracletum, deductorem scilicet omnis veritatis, unicum quidem Deum credimus, sub hac tamen dispensatione quam οἰκονομίαν dicimus, ut unici Dei sit et filius sermo ipsius, qui ex ipso processerit, per quem omnia facta sunt, et sine quo factum est nihil. Hunc missum a patre in virginem et ex ea natum, hominem et Deum, filium hominis et filium Dei, et cognominatum Jesum Christum; hunc passum, hunc mortuum et sepultum, secundum scripturas, et resuscitatum a patre, et in coelo resumptum sedere ad dexteram patris, venturum judicare vivos et mortuos; qui exinde miserit, secundum promissionem suam, a patre spiritum sanctum paracletum, sanctificatorem fidei eorum qui credunt in patrem et filium et spiritum sanctum." *De Praescriptione*, 13 : "Regula est autem fidei, ut jam hinc quid defendamus profiteamur, illa scilicet qua creditur unum omnino Deum esse nec alium praeter mundi conditorem, qui universa de nihilo produxerit per verbum suum primo omnium demissum; id verbum filium ejus appellatum, in nomine Dei varie visum a patriarchis, in prophetis semper auditum, postremo delatum ex spiritu patris Dei et virtute in virginem Mariam, carnem factum in utero ejus, et ex ea natum exisse Jesum Christum; exinde predicasse novam legem et novam promissionem regni coelorum, virtutes fecisse, cruci fixum tertia die resurrexisse, in coelos ereptum sedisse ad dexteram patris, mississe vicariam vim spiritus sancti qui credentes agat, venturum cum claritate ad sumendos sanctos in vitae aeternae et promissorum coelestium fructum, et ad profanos judicandos igni perpetuo, facta utriusque partis resuscitatione cum carnis restitutione."

*De Praescriptione*, 36 : " Si autem Italiæ adjaces, habes Romam, unde nobis quoque auctoritas præsto est . . . Videamus quid didicerit, quid docuerit, cum Africanis quoque ecclesiis contesserarit. Unum Deum dominum novit, creatorem universitatis, et Christum Jesum ex virgine Maria filium dei creatoris, et carnis resurrectionem."

Comparing these passages with the tentative reconstruction of Irenæus' creed given on p. 50 seq., we find in the first place that Irenæus and Tertullian agree in the following variations from the fourth century text of R.

1. They both have ἕνα before θεόν in article 1.

This may have stood in the original text of R, as Zahn maintains over against Harnack and Kattenbusch (see Zahn, *Das apostolische Symbolum*, p. 22 seq., and also Burn, *An Introduction to the Creeds*, p. 55 seq.), and the following passage from *Adv. Prax.*, 3, seems at first sight conclusive evidence of it: "The simple ... are startled at the οἰκονομία, on the ground that the very rule of faith withdraws them from the world's many gods to the one only and true God (*ad unicum et verum deum*)." But *verum* is not in Tertullian's creed in any case and the article *in deum patrem omnipotentem* might be sufficient to justify the position of the "simple," for it implies one only and true God. If ἕνα did not stand in the original creed it would be very natural for Irenæus to insert it in his conflict with the Gnostics, whose fundamental error was their assumption of two gods, just as in some passages he inserted ἕνα before Χριστὸν Ἰησοῦν; and as Tertullian was directly under Irenæus' influence, and was combating the same heretics, he might be expected to follow him in the matter. It is to be noticed that Tertullian has *unum* in two of the passages quoted and *unicum* in the others, while the Latin version of Irenæus, which was familiar to Tertullian, has uniformly *unum*. This variation suggests that the word may not have been securely fixed in the creed. It is to be noticed also that the later omission of ἕνα in R and in all the North African and Gallic creeds is very difficult to explain if it constituted a part of the creed in the beginning. Zahn (followed by Burn) ascribes the omission to the influence of Patripassianism, but the cure in that case would be worse than the disease, for the deliberate expunging of the word would seem to show that the church did not believe in one God as it always insisted that it did. On the whole, it seems to me altogether probable that ἕνα was not in the original text of R, but represents, like *creator*, etc., an addition of Irenæus and Tertullian.

2. Both Irenæus and Tertullian have phrases and clauses in the first article referring to God as creator. The expressions used by Irenæus are given above on p. 50. In Tertullian we have "mundi conditorem" (*De Virg. Vel.*, 1); "mundi conditorem, qui universa de nihilo produxerit per verbum suum" (*De Praescriptione*, 13); "creatorem universitatis" (*De Praescriptione*, 36). The words vary widely in both writers, and are without doubt additions to the original text of R, made by them in their conflict with the Gnostics.

3. Irenæus and Tertullian both use a passive participle (Irenæus, *receptus* and the noun ἀνάληψις; Tertullian, *receptus*, *resumptus*, *ereptus*) in referring to the ascension, while R has the active ἀναβάντα (*ascendit*). But the same word is not used by Irenæus and Tertullian in every case, and as in the New Testament references to the ascension a passive verb is used (ἀνελήμφθη, Mark XVI. 19, Acts I. 2, 11, 22; ἀνεφέρετο, Luke XXIV. 51; ἐπήρθη, Acts I. 9) it seems probable that R had the active ἀναβάντα which Irenæus, followed by Tertullian, changed to the passive under the influence of the

New Testament. The point is of small importance, and no positive conclusion can be reached, but it is easier to explain this change than the opposite.

4. In both Irenæus and Tertullian μονογενής is wanting in the second article; and as both believe that Christ is μονογενής (*unigenitus*), and use the word frequently in connection with him, and as there is no apparent reason for omitting the word in their reproductions of the creed if it actually constituted a part of the symbol, we may fairly conclude that it was not in the creed used by them and so not in the original text of R. The word is also omitted in some western recensions of R (see Hahn, §§ 40, 48, 51, 53, 57, 61, 70), but the omission even where textually certain, as it is not in the first four (cf. Kattenbusch, I. p. 110, 138, 150, 157), has little significance owing to the composite origin or late date of the texts in question (cf. *ibid.*, p. 399, 158, 181). The word is wanting too in the creed of the Syriac *Didascalia*, of the third century, if Zahn's conjectural reconstruction of it is to be relied upon (see his *Neuere Beiträge zur Geschichte des apostolischen Symbolums* in the *Neue Kirchliche Zeitschrift*, 1896, p. 22 seq.). Zahn also thinks that μονογενής was not a part of the original text of R and suggests (*Das apostolische Symbolum*, p. 45) that the word was inserted in the time of Zephyrinus, when according to his view ἕνα was

omitted from the first article and πατερα added to it.

5. In both Tertullian and Irenæus τὸν κύριον ἡμῶν is wanting in the second article; and though, as was remarked on p. 51, the phrase may have constituted a part of the creed as known to Irenæus, its omission by Tertullian in all his statements of the creed makes it probable that it did not, but was added later, as was the case with various other phrases.

6. Ἐκ πνεύματος ἁγίου is wanting in the third article both in Irenæus and Tertullian. But in the second of the passages quoted just above from Tertullian (*Adv. Prax.*, 2) we have: *missum a patre in virginem et ex ea natum;* and in the third (*De Praescriptione*, 13): *delatum ex spiritu patris dei et virtute in virginem Mariam;* and in *Adv. Marc.*, V. 17 we have *natum ex virgine dei spiritu* (cf. also *De Carne Christi,* passim). The wide variations in form in these and many others of Tertullian's references to the agency of the Holy Spirit in connection with the birth of Christ go to confirm the conclusion suggested by their omission in *De Virg. Vel.*, 1 and *De Praescriptione*, 36, that the words *de Spiritu Sancto* did not form a part of the creed used by him, and as they are not testified to by Irenæus, it may fairly be assumed that they were not in the original text of R. This assumption is still further strengthened by the fact that the reference to the

agency of the Holy Spirit in connection with the birth of Jesus is lacking also in the creeds of Lucian the Martyr (see Hahn, §§ 129 and 156, and Kattenbusch, I. p. 252 seq. and 262 seq.), of Antioch (Hahn, § 130; Kattenbusch, I. p. 220 seq.), and of Laodicea (Hahn, § 131; cf. Kattenbusch, I. p. 223), — a fact which makes it altogether probable that they were lacking in the original symbol of Syria-Palestine, which there is good reason for thinking was based upon R (see below, p. 103). It is perhaps worth noting in this connection that both Hippolytus and Origen, the former of whom certainly and the latter possibly knew R as it existed early in the third century, in referring to the virgin birth mention Mary first and the Spirit afterward (see Kattenbusch, II. p. 141 and 358). It is not impossible that there is a hint here that R at that time contained no mention of the agency of the Spirit or that the reference had been recently added and the form of the article was not yet securely fixed.[1]

7. The article on the Holy Church is wanting both in Irenæus and Tertullian. In his tract on Baptism, chapter 6, Tertullian says "Cum autem sub tribus et testatio fidei et sponsio salutis pigne-

[1] The creed of the Marcionite Apelles, as reconstructed by Harnack (see above, p. 69), has ἀπὸ Μαρίας τῆς παρθένου, but no reference to the Spirit. If the creed was based upon R, as Harnack thinks, it may be used as another witness against the presence of the phrase ἐκ πνεύματος ἁγίου in the original text.

rentur, necessario adjicitur ecclesiæ mentio, quoniam ubi tres, id est Pater et Filius et Spiritus Sanctus, ibi ecclesia, quae trium corpus est." These words are commonly taken to prove that the Old Roman Symbol contained an article on the church in the time of Tertullian. In Tertullian's various statements of the creed no such article occurs, and the same is true of Irenæus. It is of course possible that the creed they used contained the article in question ($\dot{\alpha}\gamma\iota\alpha\nu$ $\dot{\epsilon}\kappa\kappa\lambda\eta\sigma\iota\alpha\nu$, as in the fourth century text of R, or simply $\dot{\epsilon}\kappa\kappa\lambda\eta\sigma\iota\alpha\nu$, which is the most that Tertullian implies in *De Bapt.*, 6), and that both Irenæus and Tertullian omitted it in their statements of the creed because it was of no particular importance to them. But on the other hand it is equally possible that in speaking of the church in *De Bapt.*, 6, Tertullian was not thinking of the creed, and that the mention of the church with the names of Father, Son and Spirit had nothing to do with the creed. If the church was thus mentioned in connection with Father, Son, and Spirit as the representative of God on earth or the earthly embodiment of the divine (*quoniam ubi tres, id est Pater et Filius et Spiritus Sanctus, ibi ecclesia, quae trium corpus est*), it would be natural for an article upon the church to make its way later into the creed. Such an article was already in it at the time of Cyprian, but there it has the peculiar form *in remissionem peccatorum et vitam aeternam per sanctam ecclesiam*, a form which persisted for some time in North Africa (see Hahn, §§ 47, 48, 49). In this particular case it is easier to understand the addition of the article in the early third century, when there was much controversy touching the nature of the church, than its insertion at the time of the composition of the creed, fifty or seventy-five years earlier. Under the circumstances it would seem that the possibility must be recognized that the article on the church in the fourth century text of R may be a third century addition, like the article on the remission of sins, the word μονογενής and the phrase ἐκ πνεύματος ἁγίου. It may be added that the article on the church is apparently wanting in the creed of the *Didascalia* mentioned above on p. 90.

8. The article on the remission of sins is also wanting in both Irenæus' and Tertullian's reproductions of the creed, and there is consequently good reason for supposing that it too was lacking in the original text of R. The article is wanting likewise in the creed of the *Didascalia*. It should also be added that Origen in his reproductions of the Rule of Faith nowhere refers to the remission of sins (see Kattenbusch, II. p. 717). If he knew R, as maintained by Kattenbusch, his failure to mention this article may go to confirm the lack of it in the original text of R.

In the second place Tertullian disagrees with Irenæus and agrees with the fourth century text of R in the following particulars:

1. Tertullian has *crucifixus* in the fourth article in the passages quoted above from *De Virg. Vel.*, 1, and *De Praescriptione*, 13, while Irenæus has *passus*. It is true that Tertullian has *passus* instead of *crucifixus* in *Adv. Prax.*, 2, but in that passage he adds *mortuum et sepultum secundum scripturas*, which was certainly not in his creed nor in R. And so the occurrence of *passus* in this passage cannot be taken as evidence of its presence in R. Moreover, it is to be noticed that Irenæus' theological interest is such that *passus* receives great emphasis in his writings, and so it is easy to explain its substitution for *crucifixus* in his reproductions of the creed (as he substitutes it for *mortuus* in his quotations from Paul in III. 17: 9 and III. 19: 3), much easier than to explain the substitution of *crucifixus* for an original *passus*. It may therefore be concluded that the fourth century text of R is true to the original form in reading *crucifixus* instead of *passus*.

2. In the fourth article, Tertullian in one passage (*Adv. Prax.*, 2; cf. also *De Carne Christi*, 5) agrees with the fourth century text of R in giving the word *sepultus* which is omitted by Irenæus. It is true that the word *mortuus* which precedes and the phrase *secundum scripturas* which follows

(neither of which is in the fourth century text of R) suggest that the occurrence of *sepultus* here is due to the influence of 1 Cor. XV. 4 rather than of R. But in *De Carne Christi*, 5, we have also *crucifixus* ("crucifixus est dei filius ... et mortuus est dei filius ... et sepultus resurrexit") which is not in 1 Cor. XV. 4. Moreover, the word *sepultus* in itself is so insignificant that it is very difficult to account for its insertion in R without the *mortuus* with which it is connected in 1 Cor. XV. 4, if it was not originally a part of R; while, on the other hand, it is easy to understand its omission by Irenæus, and by Tertullian in most of his reproductions of the symbol, because of its apparent insignificance. We shall see when we come to the interpretation of the creed that there may have been good reason for the use of the word in the original text of R, a reason which was lacking at a later date. Under these circumstances we may fairly conclude that it was a part of the original R.[1]

3. In the first three passages quoted above Tertullian has a reference to the "session" of Christ which is wanting in Irenæus' formulations of the

---

[1] It should be added, as possibly a further confirmation of the presence of *sepultus* in the original text of R, that the creed of Apelles, according to Harnack (see above p. 69), contained a reference to the burial as well as to the crucifixion and resurrection: καὶ ἐσταυρώθη ἐν ἀληθείᾳ καὶ ἐτάφη ἐν ἀληθείᾳ καὶ ἀνέστησεν ἐν ἀληθείᾳ.

creed; and in each case the phrase used is identical with that found in the fourth century text of R: *ad dexteram patris*. It might be thought that the article was added to the original text of R by Tertullian under the influence of the New Testament, but it is to be noticed that it does not occur there in this form. Instead of πατρός we have in the New Testament δυνάμεως or θεοῦ. The phrase ἐν δεξιᾷ τοῦ πατρός occurs before Tertullian only in Irenæus III. 16: 9 (*in dextera patris*), and though there is no formal creed in that passage the occurrence of the phrase is significant, for just above Irenæus has quoted Rom. VIII. 34, in which are found the words ἐν δεξιᾷ τοῦ Θεοῦ. The change from θεός to πατήρ may well have been due to the influence of a familiar formula, and that formula may well have been R. Under these circumstances there can be little doubt that *ad dexteram patris* (ἐν δεξιᾷ τοῦ πατρός) constituted a part of the original text of R.

4. Tertullian gives the return of Christ for judgment, in the first two passages quoted above, in the simple form which it has in the fourth century text of R: *venturum judicare vivos et mortuos*. In the third passage (*De Praescriptione*, 13) he has a much more elaborate reference to the second coming which agrees in substance with the parallel statements in Irenæus, but is not verbally identical with any of them. It seems altogether

probable in view of the greater simplicity of the article as found in the fourth century text of R and in the two passages of Tertullian, and in view of the variations in the article as reproduced by Irenæus, that the former represents the original text and that Irenæus' statements contain his own theological reflections. That Irenæus should have worked his theological reflections into the creed at this point, as also at some other points, is entirely natural, for he was interested always to emphasize the salvation or real redemption of man by Christ. On the other hand, it would be exceedingly difficult to understand the later omission from the creed of the references to salvation which we find in Irenæus if they constituted originally a part of the symbol. The conclusion that the fourth century text of R represents the original form of this article is still further confirmed by the occurrence of the exact phraseology of R in a fragment from Irenæus' work *On the Ogdoad* quoted by Eusebius, *Hist. Eccles.* V. 20: 2, where we have the words ἔρχεται κρῖναι ζῶντας καὶ νεκρούς. These precise words are not found in the New Testament or in the writings of the Fathers before Irenæus. In 2 Tim. IV. 1 and Barnabas 7, we have μέλλων (μέλλοντος) κρίνειν ζῶντας καὶ νεκρούς; in Polycarp 2, ἔρχεται κρίτης ζώντων καὶ νεκρῶν; in Acts X. 42 and Justin, *Dial.* 118, κρίτης ζώντων καὶ νεκρῶν (cf. also 1 Pet. IV. 5 and 2 Clement 1).

In the third place Tertullian disagrees both with the fourth century text of R and with Irenæus in the omission of *patrem* in the first article of the creed. Taking Tertullian alone we should say that *patrem* was not in the creed known to him; and this is maintained by Zahn, *Das apostolische Symbolum*, p. 27 sq. But Irenæus confirms its presence in the original text of R, for it is to be noticed that there is no apparent reason for the insertion of the word by Irenæus if it did not constitute a part of the creed which he was using. He thought of God as the father of Christ rather than of the universe, and so the term πατήρ was not natural to him in connection with παντοκράτωρ and ποιητής. And yet he so uses it in I. 10: 1, where we find the exact phrase of R (θεὸν πατέρα παντοκράτορα). On the other hand, it is not impossible to explain the omission of *patrem* by Tertullian in his reproductions of the creed, for like Irenæus he thought of God as father in relation to Christ, not to the universe, and especially in his controversy with the Patripassianists he must find πατὴρ παντοκράτωρ awkward. Still further, there are in *Adv. Prax.* 1, 2, 9, and in *De Corona*, 3, possible hints of the presence of πατέρα in the creed known to Tertullian, and it should be added that the word is found in all the other North African forms of the symbol. Finally, it is much more difficult to account for the insertion of the word πατέρα in immediate juxtaposition to παντοκράτορα in the third century after the word had come to be used chiefly of the relation of God to Christ than in the middle of the second century, when the term was very commonly used to denote God's relation to the universe. Taking all things into consideration, it seems to me practically certain that πατέρα was in the original creed, and that its omission by Tertullian was due to the special theological interest which controlled him. (Compare upon this point Harnack, *Zeitschrift für Theologie und Kirche*, 1894, p. 130 seq., and Kattenbusch II. p. 87 seq., both of whom maintain over against Zahn that πατέρα was in the original text of R).

In the light of this comparison of the testimony of Irenæus and Tertullian with the fourth century text of R we may with more or less confidence reconstruct the original text as follows:

πιστεύω εἰς θεὸν πατέρα παντοκράτορα· καὶ εἰς Χριστὸν Ἰησοῦν τὸν υἱὸν αὐτοῦ, τὸν γεννηθέντα ἐκ Μαρίας τῆς παρθένου, τὸν ἐπὶ Ποντίου Πιλάτου σταυρωθέντα καὶ ταφέντα, τῇ τρίτῃ ἡμέρᾳ ἀναστάντα ἐκ νεκρῶν, ἀναβάντα εἰς τοὺς οὐρανούς, καθήμενον ἐν δεξιᾷ τοῦ πατρός, ὅθεν ἔρχεται κρῖναι ζῶντας καὶ νεκρούς· καὶ εἰς πνεῦμα ἅγιον, σαρκὸς ἀνάστασιν.

## IV

### THE PLACE OF COMPOSITION OF THE OLD ROMAN SYMBOL

THAT Rome was the centre from which R made its way throughout the western church is admitted by all. Tertullian testifies that his creed came from Rome (see above, p. 47) and an examination of the various western creeds given by Hahn, p. 22 seq., shows that R is the basis of them all and that the closer the connection between any church and Rome the closer the identity between its creed and R, and on the other hand the less intimate the relation the greater the divergence from R (cf. Kattenbusch, I. p. 78 seq.).

But there is a marked difference of opinion among scholars as to whether R originated in Rome itself or in the east. The former view is maintained by Harnack and Kattenbusch (see Harnack's article in the third edition of Herzog and his *Chronologie der alt-christlichen Litteratur* I. p. 524, and see Kattenbusch, II. p. 321 seq. and 960); the latter among others by Caspari (cf. his *Quellen*, Bd. III. p. 161), Zahn (*Das apostolische Symbolum*, p. 37 seq.), and most recently Sanday (*Journal of Theological Studies*, October, 1899, p. 3 seq.). Caspari seems to have made no special investigation of the question, but apparently took it for granted that R originated in the east, and because of the occurrence of μονογενής assigned it to the Johannine circle. Zahn's view is wrapped up with his contention that a symbol of which R is an outgrowth existed even in the time of the apostles. But this is utterly irreconcilable with the testimony of primitive Christian literature (see above, p. 78 seq.). Sanday's article is chiefly devoted to showing that the eastern type of creed, which in agreement with many others he regards not as a development of R itself, but as a parallel recension of an earlier eastern original, existed already before the latter part of the third century, and that therefore the suggestion of Kattenbusch that R may have found official entrance into the east in connection with the condemnation of Paul of Samosata is unsound. But to show that that suggestion is of doubtful value, or even to show that the eastern type of creed was in existence before the time in question is not to disprove the thesis that R originated in the west and was the parent of the eastern symbols as Harnack and Kattenbusch maintain, for it may easily have found its way to the east long before. However that may be — whether it is true that the eastern type was developed before the time of Paul of Samosata or not — many indications point in the direction of a western original for R. There is in the first place no trace of R or of any similar symbol in the east until at any rate well on in the third century, except in a doubtful fragment of Melito's writings (see above, p. 77), which proves nothing.[1] In the west, on the other hand, we have clear and definite testimony to the existence of R before the end of the second century.

Again, the symbol in use in Syria and Palestine at the end of the third century, which can be reconstructed in its main lines from the symbols of Cyril of Jerusalem, of Lucian and of the churches of Laodicea and Antioch (see Kattenbusch, II. p. 192 seq.), is evidently, as admitted by all, an enlargement either of R itself or of an older creed upon which R too is based, and it is noticeable that the additions to the common stock in the east are of an entirely different character from the original text, while the additions in the west whether in R or in our present Apostles' Creed are of the same nature as the original to which they are added. The western character of the parent symbol is thus strikingly shown.

On the other hand, aside from the presumption that all Christian institutions of the earliest days

---

[1] If Origen knew R, as maintained by Kattenbusch (see his careful discussion in Vol. II. p. 134 seq.), the fact proves no more, as Kattenbusch shows, than that he may have become acquainted with it during his visit to Rome in the time of Zephyrinus.

originated in the east and were carried thence to Rome — a presumption which should be allowed no weight in the present case — the only argument which can be urged in favor of an eastern origin for R is the occurrence in the oriental creeds of the fourth century of certain words and phrases which are wanting in R, but are found in Irenæus' reproductions of the symbol. Thus ἕνα with θεόν and with Χριστὸν Ἰησοῦν; ποιητής κ.τ.λ. after θεόν; παθόντα, ὑπὲρ τῆς ἡμετέρας σωτηρίας, and ὑπὲρ ἡμῶν (or διὰ ἡμάς) in the article on Christ; ἐν δόξῃ κ.τ.λ. in connection with the Second Coming. The assumption is that Irenæus brought the creed with him from the east and that his statements of it represent its eastern and original form (cf. Sanday, p. 21). But it is to be said in reply, that the phrases referred to are of such a character as to betray their later origin. They are certainly additions to R and not a part of its original text, as the theological character at any rate of most of them plainly shows. Moreover, if they belonged originally to R, their subsequent omission is very difficult to explain.

It is quite possible that the phrases which Irenæus has in common with the eastern symbols of a later day were already current in the east and were brought thence by him without yet having been incorporated into a creed. Or it is equally possible that they took their rise with him and found their way into the eastern creed under his influence. All of them have their explanation in Irenæus' own theology or in his polemics, and it is easier to understand them as originating with him than with anybody else.

In the light of these considerations, it may fairly be concluded, in agreement with Harnack and Kattenbusch, that R originated in Rome, not in the orient.

## V

### The Purpose of the Old Roman Symbol and its Historical Interpretation

The purpose for which the Old Roman Symbol was composed cannot be finally determined until we have completed our study of its contents. But it is important before we take up the several articles in detail, to notice the situation that existed in Rome at the time the creed was framed, that we may see whether it throws any light upon the matter.

Our study has led to the conclusion that R originated in Rome about the middle of the second century, or not long thereafter. But heresy was then rife in Rome, and was causing serious alarm within the church. If a creed was framed there at that particular time, we should expect it to take some notice of the errors which were making so much trouble; and if no creed existed before, so that its formation constituted an innovation, it would be natural to see in the false teachings, which were now for the first time causing alarm, the primary reason for its composition. We come then to our study of the contents of the creed with a presumption in favor of its anti-heretical purpose. The question is, does the creed itself bear out this presumption.

The movement which was making most trouble in the church of Rome at the middle of the second century, was Marcionism, and so an anti-heretical creed framed at that time could hardly fail to take account of Marcion's teachings. The Marcionitic tenets which were most offensive to Christians in general may be gathered from Tertullian's elaborate work against Marcion. Those tenets were, first, that the God of the Christians is not the Creator and ruler of the universe, who is hard, stern, and severe, but another being, the God of redemption, who is pure love and mercy and was entirely unknown until revealed by Jesus Christ (cf. Tertullian, *Adv. Marc.*, especially Bks. I. II. and IV.; also Justin Martyr, *Apol.*, I. 26 and 58; and Irenæus, I. 27); secondly, that Jesus Christ is the son of the latter being, and not of the creator and ruler of the universe (cf. Tertullian, *ibid.*, Bks. III. IV. V. *passim*); thirdly, that God, the father of Christ, being pure love and mercy will judge no one (*ibid.*, I. 6, 26 seq.; II. 11 seq.; IV. 8, 15, 17, 19, 21 seq., 29, 35 seq.; V. 4, 7 seq., 13, 16); fourthly, that the life of Christ was that of a spirit only, and his bodily form a mere phantom (*ibid.*, I. 24; II. 28; III. 8 seq.; IV. 9 seq., 19; V. 4 seq., 13, 14, 17, 19 seq., and *De Carne Christi*, 1 seq., 5 ); and finally that the flesh of man does not rise again (*Adv. Marc.* IV. 37; V. 7, 9 seq., 14 seq., 18 seq.; *De Carne Christi*, 1; *De Resurrectione Carnis*, 1 seq.).

A creed composed in Rome at the middle of the second century, if it was framed with an antiheretical purpose, must at any rate rule out these beliefs, and so we can test the purpose of the Old Roman Symbol in their light. Let us then examine the several articles of the symbol in detail.

Πιστεύω εἰς θεὸν πατέρα παντοκράτορα.

The first article of the creed was probably formed by adding to the θεός of the baptismal formula (see p. 184), the phrase πατὴρ παντοκράτωρ. Πατήρ is used of God very frequently in the Christian literature of the second century, with the meaning of author or creator of the world or the universe. Thus for instance πατέρα καὶ κτιστὴν τοῦ σύμπαντος κόσμου, 1 Clement 19; δημιουργὸς καὶ πατὴρ τῶν αἰώνων, 1 Clement 35; πατὴρ πάντων or τῶν ὅλων (with or without δεσπότης, κύριος, or δημιουργός), Justin, *Apol.* I. 12, 32, 36, 40, 44, 46, 61, 63, 65; II. 6, 10; *Dial.* 95, 105, 108, 115, 127, 128, 140; αἰσθητῶν καὶ ἀοράτων πατήρ, Tatian, *Apol.* 4. Compare also the statement of Theophilus, *Ad Autolycum* I. 4: "God is father because he is before all things" (πατὴρ διὰ τὸ εἶναι αὐτὸν πρὸ τῶν ὅλων). Πατήρ is also used (frequently by John, Ignatius, and Justin, not so often by other writers) to express the relation of God to Christ; but this is less common than the other meaning in the period with which we are dealing, and except in the Johannine and Ignatian writings πατήρ almost never has this sense when used alone, but only when explicitly connected with Christ. It is clear, therefore, that πατήρ in R, especially in view of its connection with παντοκράτωρ, means, not the father of Christ or of the Son, but the father of the world, or the universe, that is, its creator, author, or source.

Παντοκράτωρ, a common word in the Septuagint, occurs only nine times in the New Testament (once in 2 Corinthians in a quotation from the Old Testament, and eight times in the Apocalypse), but often in the writings of the early fathers (e. g., in 1 Clement, Polycarp, Hermas, Mart. Polyc., Justin, Theophilus). It is used commonly with θεός or κύριος, with πατήρ only twice before the time of Irenæus, in Justin's *Dial.* 139 (τοῦ παντοκράτορος πατρός), and in the *Martyrdom of Polycarp*, 19 (τὸν θεὸν καὶ πατέρα παντοκράτορα). The exact phrase of R (θεὸς πατὴρ παντοκράτωρ) occurs nowhere, so far as I am aware, before Irenæus, and in Irenæus probably under the influence of R (see p. 50 seq.). The word παντοκράτωρ means, not "almighty" (*omnipotens*), but "holding" or "controlling" or "governing all things" (*omnitenens*, or *qui omnia continet*). Compare for instance, *Theophilus*, I. 4: " He is παντοκράτωρ because he holds and contains all things (τὰ πάντα κρατεῖ καὶ ἐμπεριέχει), for the heights of heaven, and the depths of the abyss, and the ends of the world are in his hands." The word, therefore, refers to the sovereignty or providence of God, and the phrase πατὴρ παντοκράτωρ expresses in the most compact possible form, the belief that God made and rules the world, that he is its father and sovereign.

The phrase subsequently added to R and found in the present text of the Apostles' Creed (*creatorem cœli et terræ*), adds nothing to the sense of the original article and really makes its meaning no more explicit, except for an age which instinctively interpreted πατήρ as referring to the first person of the Trinity, or the father of Christ. It was because the word "Father" commonly had this latter meaning in the usage of Irenæus and Tertullian that they found themselves obliged to add phrases referring explicitly to the creation, when they reproduced the *regula fidei* (see pp. 50, 89). But it is a mistake to suppose that the additions made the truth that God is the maker or source of the universe, any more clear than the term πατήρ made it to the author of R and his contemporaries. In fact the brief phrase πατὴρ παντοκράτωρ better expresses the belief in God as author and ruler of the world, than the more elaborate πατὴρ παντοκράτωρ ποιητὴς οὐρανοῦ καὶ γῆς, for the latter fixes the attention on creation very largely to the exclusion of providence (the παντοκράτωρ in this collocation meaning hardly more than *omnipotens*); while in the former the two are equally emphasized.

The choice of the rare but pregnant phrase πατὴρ παντοκράτωρ, when so many other phrases expressing God's relation to the world were in common use, cannot have been accidental; and it should not be treated as if it were used thoughtlessly and without discrimination. It is evident that this particular phrase was chosen with the distinct purpose of asserting that the Christians' God, the God believed in and worshipped by Christians, is the creator and ruler of the universe. Of course it is conceivable that this assertion may have been made without any thought of existing errors on the subject, but it is so directly opposed to the teaching of Marcion that it is difficult to avoid the conclusion that it was intended as a protest against his view.

Καὶ εἰς Χριστὸν Ἰησοῦν, τὸν υἱὸν αὐτοῦ [τὸν κύριον ἡμῶν].

Kattenbusch maintains that the word Χριστός is here used not as a proper name but as an official designation, and that it is to be taken predicatively, so that the phrase εἰς Χριστὸν Ἰησοῦν expresses the belief that Jesus is the Messiah. But certainly if that had been the author's purpose he could not well have expressed himself more blindly. The position of the words and the omission of the article with Χριστός both make such an interpretation unnatural, to say the least. Moreover, the interpretation runs counter both to the general interest and purpose of R and to the common usage of the age in which it was composed.

Kattenbusch holds that the church in which R originated was essentially a "Messias-Gemeinde," primarily interested, as Peter was at Pentecost, to maintain the Messiahship of Jesus against the unbelieving Jews. But as a matter of fact, there is not a single hint in R of any such interest; and what we know of the Church of Rome, where R was framed according to Kattenbusch, lends little support to the theory that it was dominated by that interest in the second century. If it were to be supposed that Χριστός was used by the author of R in its Jewish sense of "anointed" or "Messiah," it would be easier and more in line with the remainder of the creed to interpret it as joined with Ἰησοῦς for the purpose of asserting the identity of the historic figure Jesus with the Messiah prophesied in the Old Testament over against Marcion's denial of the identity. But the current use of the word Χριστός in the age in which R originated was such that it is altogether probable that the author of R used the word simply as a proper name with no special interest in its historic Jewish meaning. There can be no question that the word, whether with or without Ἰησοῦς, was commonly employed in that way in his day. Even in the epistles of Paul, who as a Jew would be always conscious of the original meaning of Χριστός if any one was, the word occurs far more often as a proper name than as a title. And the same is true of the post-canonical writings of the first and second centuries.

In Paul, according to the consensus of the most recent editors, Χριστός alone, more often without than with the article, occurs most frequently, but Χριστὸς Ἰησοῦς and Ἰησοῦς Χριστός each upward of sixty times. In the Apostolic fathers Ἰησοῦς Χριστός is commonest, but Χριστός alone and Χριστὸς Ἰησοῦς also occur not infrequently and apparently with no distinction in meaning. The three are used indifferently also in Irenæus, while in Justin's Apologies, according to Otto's edition, Χριστὸς Ἰησοῦς does not appear. The use of Χριστὸς Ἰησοῦς, therefore, instead of Ἰησοῦς Χριστός in R indicates only that with the author of the creed it was the common designation for Christ, or more probably that being less common it was selected as more solemn and striking. In any case its meaning in R is the same as if it were Ἰησοῦς Χριστός; it is simply a proper name to designate the historic figure Jesus Christ.

The full name Χριστὸς Ἰησοῦς, instead of Χριστός or Ἰησοῦς alone, might conceivably have been used with the special purpose of making impossible the Gnostic separation of the æon Χριστός from the human person Ἰησοῦς, thus repudiating one of the current forms of docetism, but in view of the prevalence of the double name, and of the formal character of R which would make its use here all the more natural, such special purpose must be recognized as doubtful.

The words τὸν υἱὸν αὐτοῦ are to be taken predicatively. They were added to Χριστὸν Ἰησοῦν in order to assert that the historic figure Christ Jesus is the son of the θεὸς πατὴρ παντοκράτωρ referred to in the first article. It is evidently the controlling purpose of the second article to assert belief not primarily in Christ Jesus, but in the relation that subsisted between him and the Father and Ruler of the world. Belief in Christ Jesus was involved in the very act of baptism, but the relation between him and the creator and ruler of the universe was matter of dispute.

The article taken by itself might have either of two references. It might be intended to assert Christ's divine sonship, over against the heathen denial that he was a divine messenger and the bearer of a divine revelation (cf. Justin, *Apol.* I. 24 seq.), and this interpretation would accord well with the mention of the crucifixion just below, as it was chiefly because of the crucifixion that the claims of Christ were ridiculed and rejected. On the other hand, the article might be interpreted as asserting that Christ Jesus is the son of the God who made and rules the world, over against Marcion's view that there is no connection between them, but that Christ is the son of another God altogether. (Compare the words of Tertullian in *Adv. Marc.* III. 1: "By proving Christ to be the creator's son we shut out the God of Marcion.") Read in the light of the first article and also of the creed as a whole, the latter interpretation seems to me alone allowable.

However that may be, it is evident that the article refers not to the pre-existent son of God — the divine Logos, or the second person of the Trinity — but to the historic figure Jesus. Divine sonship is asserted only of the historic person who was born of a virgin, was crucified, buried and raised again from the dead. Whether that person existed before his birth from a virgin R does not say. It does not exclude belief in such pre-existence, but on the other hand it does not assert it, nor even hint at it in the remotest way. A comparison of R with the Nicene creed and other related creeds of the third and fourth centuries is very striking in this connection. Thus the original Nicene creed reads: "One Lord Jesus Christ, the son of God, begotten from the Father, only begotten, that is from the *ousia* of the Father, God from God, Light from Light, true God from true God, begotten not made, homoousios with the Father, through whom all things were made . . . who for us men and for our salvation came down and became flesh," etc. So also the creed of Eusebius of Cæsarea reads: "One Lord Jesus Christ, the Logos of God, God from God, light from light, life from life, Son only begotten, first born of every creature, before all the æons from the Father begotten, through whom also all things were made, who for our salvation became flesh," etc.

At the time when R was framed the belief in the pre-existence of the Son of God was widespread (though not universal, as appears from Justin, *Dial*. 48), and the omission of the doctrine in R is very significant. It does not show that the author did not believe it, but it does show that he was interested here in another matter altogether. He was not concerned to say what he or the church believed in general about Christ, he could hardly have avoided some reference to the pre-existence in that case, either by way of assent or dissent, but he was concerned to assert a particular truth about Christ, which was denied by many, the truth namely that the historic figure Jesus Christ is ὁ υἱὸς θεοῦ πατρὸς παντοκράτορος. In the light of contemporary Christian literature (2 Clement, Hermas, Justin, and the other apologists) this is the only satisfactory explanation of the author's failure to refer in any way to the pre-existence of the Son.

As was seen above, p. 91, it is doubtful, in the light of the testimony of Irenæus and Tertullian, whether the phrase τὸν κύριον ἡμῶν constituted a part of the original text of R. In itself there is nothing suspicious about the phrase. The title κύριος was commonly applied to Christ by the Christian writers of the first and second centuries, and it might naturally have been inserted in R, whether the author was thinking of heathen and unbelievers or of heretics. In the former case the common contempt for Christ might well have led to an assertion of his Lordship; in the latter case it might have seemed important to make still more explicit the fact that the Christ Jesus who was declared to be the son of the God of creation and providence was not the mere Jewish Messiah whose relation to the creating God of course Marcion would have no trouble in recognizing (cf. Tertullian, *Adv. Marc.* IV. 6, V. 16), but the Christ whom all Christians, Marcion as well as others, recognized as Lord. We can thus, even on the assumption that the Creed was anti-Marcionitic in its interest, explain satisfactorily the presence of the words in the original text of R, while at the same time it is clear that the article would adequately fulfil its purpose if the words were lacking, as they possibly were.

When the words were added, if they were not in the original text, we do not know, but probably when the phrase ἐκ πνεύματος ἁγίου was inserted in the next article and under the same impulse. The addition of the words would introduce nothing new into the creed, any more than ἐκ πνεύματος ἁγίου, but both additions would indicate a change of interest and of emphasis.

Μονογενής, which apparently formed no part of the original text of R (see p 90 above), was probably added at about the same time and in the same general interest: to emphasize the uniqueness of Christ's sonship and so his exaltation above other men. Such uniqueness was unquestionably involved in the original creed. It never occurred to the author, or to any of his Christian contemporaries, to think of Christ as a son of God only in the sense in which every other man is God's son, but as the author was interested in the identity of the Father of Christ with the Father and Lord of the universe, and in the reality of the earthly life of Christ, there was no reason for emphasizing the difference between his sonship and that of other men, which indeed no one questioned. The addition of the word, which was getting into common use in the latter part of the second century, doubtless under the influence of the Fourth Gospel, was entirely natural.[1] Whether the use of the word by the Gnostics as a name for Christ (see Irenæus, *Adv. Haer.* I. 8: 5; 9: 2; III. 11: 1; IV. praef. 3; IV. 33: 3) had anything to do with it we cannot say, but it is a mistake to suppose that its insertion was for a polemical purpose, to oppose the æon doctrine of the Gnostics, which made Christ only one of a number of æons or emanations from deity; for the term was common in Gnostic circles and its application to Christ in R would have no weight over against them. Whenever it was inserted it was intended not to oppose the doctrine of æons but to emphasize the dignity of the historic person Jesus Christ, the uniqueness of his sonship when compared with that of other men. Whatever its significance in the Fourth Gospel, in R it refers not to the pre-existent son or Logos, but to the historic figure Jesus Christ, the person γεννηθέντα ἐκ πνεύματος ἁγίου καὶ Μαρίας τῆς παρθένου.

---

[1] Compare *Martyrdom of Polycarp*, 20; Justin, *Dial.* 105, and his *Syntagma*, quoted by Irenæus, IV. 6: 2; *Testament of Benjamin*, 9; Irenæus, I. 9: 2, 3; 10: 3; III. 16: 2, 6, 7, 9; III. 17: 4; IV. 5: 4; Tertullian, *Adv. Prax.* 7. The word is found, referring to Christ, nowhere in the New Testament except in the Gospel and First Epistle of John, and nowhere in the Apostolic fathers.

Τὸν γεννηθέντα ἐκ Μαρίας τῆς παρθένου· τὸν ἐπὶ Ποντίου Πιλάτου σταυρωθέντα καὶ ταφέντα, τῇ τρίτῃ ἡμέρᾳ ἀναστάντα ἐκ νεκρῶν, ἀναβάντα εἰς τοὺς οὐρανούς, καθήμενον ἐν δεξιᾷ τοῦ πατρός, ὅθεν ἔρχεται κρῖναι ζῶντας καὶ νεκρούς.

The seven items mentioned in this section of the creed — birth, crucifixion, burial, resurrection, ascension, session, and second coming — though all of them are referred to in one place or another, are found together nowhere in Christian literature before the composition of R. So far as our sources enable us to judge, the series is original with the author of R and represents a conscious selection on his part. It should throw light therefore upon the interest which governed him in the composition of the creed.

The first thing that strikes us is the large number of omissions. The author passes directly from the birth to the crucifixion without any reference to Christ's Davidic lineage, or to the fact that he has fulfilled the Scriptures (omissions which are fatal to Kattenbusch's interpretation of the creed as controlled by the Messianic interest), and without any reference to his baptism, his sinless life, his teaching, his revelation of God's will and truth, his works of mercy and of power, his victory over demons, the kingdom which he came to found, his significance as a

Saviour, and the purpose of his death. All these matters are made much of in the Christian writings of the first and second centuries, and their omission demands an explanation. That they were not omitted for brevity's sake simply is clear from the fact that other things of less moment and less frequently referred to in the literature of the period find a place in the symbol, for instance the burial and the ascension. It cannot have been mere accident or mere desire to make the creed as short as possible that led to the omission of the most important of all truths in the eyes of the Christians of that day, that Christ had brought a knowledge of God's will and truth, that he was a Saviour, and that he had died "for our sins" or "for us." If the purpose of the creed was to summarize the faith of the church touching Christ and his work; if it had an historical, or an evangelical, or a catechetical purpose, if it was intended to put before new converts, or disciples in general the fundamental facts and truths of the Gospel, it could not have omitted all it did. Nor if its purpose was apologetic, to defend Christ and Christianity against the attacks of heathen and unbelievers, could it have passed altogether Christ's character, and his wonderful works, including his subjection of demons, which was still manifested in the exorcism of evil spirits by the mere mention of his name. (Compare the Apologies of Justin, who makes a great deal of Christ's victory over the demons.)

The only plausible explanation of the many and striking omissions would seem to be that the author of R was concerned simply to repudiate certain false views about Christ which were causing particular trouble at the time he wrote, and omitted everything which was not immediately related thereto. Is this explanation borne out by the facts? Let us take up the items severally and in detail.

Τὸν γεννηθέντα ἐκ Μαρίας τῆς παρθένου.

The words ἐκ πνεύματος ἁγίου were wanting in the original text of R as shown on p. 91 above. The phrase ἐκ Μαρίας τῆς παρθένου of course carried with it by implication the uniqueness and miraculousness of Christ's birth, in which the author certainly believed, but it is clear that he was interested not in the miraculousness but in the reality of the birth, as Ignatius also was (cf., e. g. *Smyrn.* 1). If it had been its miraculous character that interested him, if it had been the divineness of Christ's origin that he was concerned to emphasize, he could not have contented himself with the simple phrase quoted above. If the words ἐκ πνεύματος ἁγίου constituted a part of the original text there might be ground for thinking that the author wished to emphasize Christ's divine origin, though even then we could not be sure of it; but in the absence of those words it is impossible to think so. He evidently wished to assert that Christ was actually born — a fact which was denied by Marcion, who held that he came down suddenly from heaven a full-grown man — and that his earthly life was therefore a reality, which Marcion also denied.

The use of the preposition ἐκ is to be noticed in this connection. Ignatius, who is very persistent in his emphasis upon the reality of Christ's earthly life over against docetism, has the same preposition (*Trall.*, 9; *Smyrn.*, 1), while Justin, who has a great deal to say about the pre-existence of Christ, and is more concerned to maintain his divinity than the reality of his earthly life, commonly uses the preposition διά in speaking of the Virgin birth. But διά makes it easier to look upon the birth, as the Valentinians for instance did, as unreal, and as meaning only the passage of a pre-existent being through the womb of the Virgin, without actually becoming man or assuming human flesh (cf. Irenæus, I. 7, 2, and Tertullian, *De Carne Christi*, 30). The preposition ἐκ, on the other hand, makes any such interpretation impossible. Whether διά was consciously rejected in favor of ἐκ by the author of R, as it was by Irenæus and Tertullian, we do not know, but at any rate ἐκ serves to bring out clearly the reality of the birth as διά would not have done.

That R says only γεννηθέντα, while Ignatius makes the statement more emphatic by the use of the adverb ἀληθῶς — "truly" — is no argument against the polemic interest of the article in R. The simple statement of R taken by itself is just as decisive and unequivocal as the more emphatic statement of Ignatius, and whether one shall say "was truly born" is purely a question of style. If the author of R had had before him the statements of Ignatius and had purposely omitted the ἀληθῶς there might be some significance in its omission, but there is no sign that he had.

The reality of Christ's birth might have been stated in more general terms than are used in R, for instance ἐκ γυναικός ("of a woman:" cf. Gal. IV. 4); but the phrase as it stands makes the fact much more definite and carries with it the acceptance of the account of Christ's birth in the first and third gospels, which Marcion rejected altogether. The mere statement of a general belief that Christ was born somewhere and at some time would be far less effective and thoroughgoing in its repudiation of Marcion's position than the explicit declaration that he was born of the particular woman named in the gospels, and in the common Christian tradition. It is to be noticed that it is not said γεννηθέντα ἐκ παρθένου — "born of a virgin" — which might point to a peculiar interest in the virginity of Christ's mother (as for instance in most of Justin's references to Christ's birth), but γεννηθέντα ἐκ Μαρίας τῆς παρθένου — "born of Mary the Virgin" — which shows that the author wished simply to identify her. The phrase "Mary the Virgin," or "The Virgin Mary," was not, so far as we can judge, a common phrase among the early Christians. In fact it does not occur in the New Testament, nor is it found in Christian literature prior to the formation of R except twice in Justin's *Dialogue*, chapter 100: Μαρία ἡ παρθένος, and chapter 120: διὰ τῆς παρθένου Μαρίας. Although Justin refers to the virgin birth some thirty times he mentions the name Mary only in these two passages and in *Dial.* 78. The phrase of R therefore must have been deliberately chosen, and, as already remarked, doubtless with the purpose of identifying the mother of Christ and so making the reference to his birth more definite and explicit.

It is evident that this article, with its emphasis upon the reality of Christ's birth and not upon the uniqueness of it, cannot have been directed against heathen and unbelievers, for they would never have thought of questioning the fact that Christ was actually born; and it is difficult to regard it as a mere positive statement of the Christian faith uttered without thought of heresy or error, for it could hardly have occurred to a Christian to emphasize the fact that Christ was really born except in reply to the denial of it. The article, therefore, as it stands in the original text with the emphasis on the reality of Christ's birth, cannot be satisfactorily explained, except as a protest against docetism, and more particularly the docetism of Marcion. And so any one who believed that Christ was really born, and that his life was not a mere phantom, even though he did not believe that Christ was born of a virgin, was in accord with the spirit of the article though not with its form.

The phrase ἐκ πνεύματος ἁγίου, which was probably inserted late in the second or early in the third century, really adds nothing to the article, for the birth from the Virgin carried with it the agency of the Spirit as recounted in Matthew and Luke; but it transfers the emphasis from the reality of Christ's birth to his divine origin, and so marks a change of interest. It is of a piece with the additions in the previous article μονογενής and τὸν κύριον ἡμῶν (if the latter was an addition), and indicates the same desire to emphasize the dignity and worth of Christ, which were equally recognized by the author of the original text, but which his purpose in composing the creed made it unnecessary to lay stress upon.

The virgin birth was widely though not universally believed at the time R was composed. It is mentioned nowhere in the New Testament, except in the infancy sections of the gospels of Matthew and Luke, nor is it referred to by any of the Apostolic Fathers, except Ignatius who speaks of it twice (*Eph.* 19, *Smyrn.* 1). But the apologist Aristides mentions it (*Apol.* 2), and Justin Martyr has a great deal to say about it (see *Apol.* I. 21, 22, 31, 32, 33, 46, 54; II. 6; *Dial.* 23, 43, 45, 48, 54, 57, 63, 66, 67, 68, 70, 71, 75, 76, 78, 84, 85, 87, 100, 101, 105, 127), and from his time on there is no lack of reference to it. It is clear that it was a common belief in Justin's day, but there were still some Christians that did not accept it, as appears from *Dial.* 48.

The early stages of the belief we cannot trace. It can hardly have originated with Matthew or Luke, upon the basis of whose accounts it became a part of the faith of the church (cf. Justin, *Apol.* I. 33; *Dial.* 78, 84, 100, 105), for it does not dominate nor does it even color their story of Christ's life. In fact, it stands entirely isolated in both gospels. In the form which it has in them, it is quite different from the belief in the pre-existence of Christ, which was shared by Paul and John, and must have originated independently of it. For what we have in Matthew and Luke is not the incarnation of a pre-existent being, but the origin of a new being. It is not that the Holy Spirit (or the Logos) passes through the womb of Mary and so becomes a man, but that the Holy Spirit joins with Mary in producing a new person, Jesus Christ (cf. Ménégoz, *La Théologie de l'Epître aux Hébreux*, p. 91). And so the belief in the virgin birth and the belief in the pre-existence and deity of Christ do not depend historically the one upon the other.

When these two independent beliefs — the pre-existence of Christ and the virgin birth — both became current, they were reconciled, apparently without any thought of a possible inconsistency between them, by interpreting the accounts in Matthew and Luke as a description of the method by which the pre-existent Logos or Son of God became incarnate (cf. for instance Justin Martyr, *Apol.* I. 33, 46; *Dial.* 75, 84, 85, 87, 100, 105; and the fathers in general after his time; and compare also the Nicene Creed). Of this reconciliation there is no sign in R. Indeed, we have in R no hint of pre-existence, and so no reconciliation is needed. The author very likely believed in Christ's pre-existence, but so far as the creed goes we have the standpoint of Matthew and Luke represented, not the standpoint of Justin and those who came after him. Evidently, as already remarked, it was not the virgin birth as such in which the author of R was chiefly interested — living when he did he could hardly have failed in that case to reveal his attitude toward the doctrine of pre-existence — but the reality of the birth.

Τὸν ἐπὶ Ποντίου Πιλάτου σταυρωθέντα καὶ ταφέντα, τῇ τρίτῃ ἡμέρᾳ ἀναστάντα ἐκ νεκρῶν.

No Christian symbol, whatever its purpose, could well have omitted to mention the death and resurrection of Christ, the two events in his career which bulked more largely than any others in the eyes of his disciples. It might seem unnecessary therefore to seek for any other explanation of the reference to these events. If the anti-heretical purpose of the creed called for an allusion to Christ at all and especially to the fact of his birth, his death and resurrection could not well be passed over even though the mention of them served no polemic interest.

But on the other hand the particular form of the articles in question, the reference to the seemingly unimportant fact of the burial, and the general character of the creed as a whole suggest that there may have been some special reason for the mention in the Old Roman Symbol of the crucifixion and the resurrection as well as of the birth. And first let us look at the article on the crucifixion: τὸν ἐπὶ Ποντίου Πιλάτου σταυρωθέντα, *who under* (or *in the time of*) *Pontius Pilate was crucified*. The article appears in this form prior to the composition of R only in the writings of Justin Martyr (e. g., *Apol.* I. 13, 61; II. 6; *Dial.* 30, 76, 85), and there σταυρωθέντα always precedes ἐπὶ Ποντίου Πιλάτου. The full name Pontius Pilate is found in Christian literature before R in Luke III. 1; Acts IV. 27; 1 Tim. VI. 13; Ignatius, *Magn.* 11, *Trall.* 9, *Smyrn.* 1, and frequently in Justin. The whole clause occurs repeatedly in Justin as part of a formula of exorcism (see above, p. 72) and it is possible that the phrase ἐπὶ Ποντίου Πιλάτου came into R under the influence of its use in that connection, the clause as we have it in R representing merely a stereotyped way of referring to the crucifixion, and meaning no more to the author than σταυρωθέντα alone. But in view of the compactness of R and also in view of the emphatic position of the words ἐπὶ Ποντίου Πιλάτου it is much more likely that those words, whether known to the author as part of a formula of exorcism or not, were inserted with a definite purpose. Both in Ignatius and in Justin we find them used in order to fix definitely the historic fact of the crucifixion, and in Ignatius (*Magn.* 11, *Trall.* 9, *Smyrn.* 1) this is done with a special view to the Docetists who were denying the reality of Christ's life and death. It is possible that it was for the same purpose that the author of R used the words in question. It is interesting to notice that Rufinus in his commentary on the Apostles' Creed, written at the beginning of the fifth century (chap. 18), says that the phrase *sub Pontio Pilato* " means the time when these things were done so that the tradition should not falter as though vague and uncertain."

The word ταφέντα — *buried* — makes the reality of the crucifixion still more emphatic and renders a docetic view of it still more impossible. Compare for instance the use of the word by Peter in Acts II. 29, in connection with the death of David, and compare also Tertullian, *De Carne Christi* 5. That the crucifixion was not a mere sham or show, is proved by the fact that Christ Jesus was not simply crucified but buried. The fact of the burial taken by itself is unimportant, and it is difficult to see why a reference to it should have been inserted in so compact a creed as R if the purpose was simply a positive summary of the Christian faith. Outside of the accounts in the gospels the burial of Christ is mentioned only four times in the New Testament, in Paul's speech at Antioch of Pisidia, Acts XIII. 29 (καθελόντες ἀπὸ τοῦ ξύλου ἔθηκαν εἰς μνημεῖον), in Rom. VI. 4, and Col. II. 12, where the believer is said to be "buried with Christ" in baptism (συνετάφημεν or συνταφέντες αὐτῷ), and in 1 Cor. XV. 4 (καὶ ἐτάφη). It is not mentioned in any other Christian writings prior to the time of the composition of R except once in the Apology of Aristides (chap. 2), and twice in the *Dialogue* of Justin (chaps. 97 and 118), in neither case in connection with the crucifixion or as part of a formula. In the light of the few references to it in early Christian literature its occurrence in R is very striking. It might perhaps be thought that Paul's allusion to it in 1 Cor. XV. 4, in his brief summary of the faith handed down to him, accounts for its insertion in R. But it is to be noticed that Paul connects it with ἀπέθανεν, not with ἐσταυρώθη, and moreover that he says much more which R omits (Χριστὸς ἀπέθανεν ὑπὲρ τῶν ἁμαρτιῶν ἡμῶν κατὰ τὰς γραφάς . . . καὶ ὅτι ἐγήγερται [ἐγείρω instead of the ἀνίστημι of R] τῇ ἡμέρᾳ τῇ τρίτῃ κατὰ τὰς γραφάς, καὶ ὅτι ὤφθη Κηφᾷ κ.τ.λ), while he omits the crucifixion and ascension which are found in R. Under these circumstances it is hardly possible that ταφέντα occurs in R because the author was following 1 Cor. XV. 4. On the contrary, the use of the word can be satisfactorily accounted for only on the assumption of an anti-docetic interest.

The article on the resurrection appears in the form it has in R nowhere else prior to the composition of the Old Roman Symbol. The nearest approach to it is in Justin, *Dial.* 51, 76, and 100, where we have τῇ τρίτῃ ἡμέρᾳ ἀναστάντα, without ἐκ νεκρῶν.

The phrase τῇ τρίτῃ ἡμέρᾳ (or τῇ ἡμέρᾳ τῇ τρίτῃ, as it is in Luke XVIII. 33 and 1 Cor. XV. 4) occurs three times in Matthew with ἐγείρω, twice in Luke with ἀνίστημι (once possibly with ἐγείρω), once in Acts and once in 1 Corinthians, both times with ἐγείρω. In Mark we have uniformly μετὰ τρεῖς ἡμέρας, in each case with ἀνίστημι. Though the resurrection of Christ is referred to very frequently, the "third day" is not mentioned elsewhere in Christian literature prior to R except in Justin's *Dialogue,* where it occurs five times, always with ἀνίστημι (*Dial.* 51, 76, 97, 100, 107). The phrase in the form μετὰ τρεῖς ἡμέρας was probably used originally to emphasize the brevity of the time between Christ's death and resurrection (cf. my *Apostolic Age*, p. 37, note), but outside of the gospels it appears simply as a stereotyped phrase, with no special significance, except in Justin's *Dialogue*, (chap. 107), where it is connected with the "three days" of Jonah; and perhaps Paul had this in mind when he said κατὰ τὰς γραφάς (1 Cor. XV. 4).

In the light of its use in early Christian literature it is evident that the phrase may have been used in R simply as part of a stereotyped formula, without any special meaning attaching to it, but in view of the same considerations that were urged in connection with ἐπὶ Ποντίου Πιλάτου (the compactness of R, and the emphatic position of the phrase in question), it seems probable that the author inserted the words with the definite purpose of making the fact of the resurrection more real by stating precisely the time at which it occurred. Not merely did Christ rise at some indefinite time, but "on the third day." The reference was very likely intended also to carry with it the acceptance of the account in the Gospels and so the repudiation of the idea of a mere spiritual resurrection.

It has been suggested that the interval of three days was mentioned in order to make certain the reality of the death of Christ by excluding the supposition of a mere swoon or trance; but so far as I am aware the phrase was never used in the early church to emphasize length of time, and there is no sign of such a use of it here.

The resurrection is referred to in primitive Christian literature both within and without the New Testament either by the single word ἀνίστημι or ἐγείρω, or by the full phrase ἀνίστημι (or ἐγείρω) ἐκ νεκρῶν (less often ἀπὸ τῶν νεκρῶν), and apparently without any difference in meaning or emphasis (cf., e. g., Ignatius, *Trall.* 9 and *Smyrn.* 2). The words ἐκ νεκρῶν in R, therefore, are perhaps without any special significance, the phrase ἀναστάντα ἐκ νεκρῶν meaning no more than ἀναστάντα alone. At the same time it is possible that the author added them purposely in order to render still more emphatic the reality of the resurrection. It was not that Christ Jesus appeared to his disciples out of heaven, whither he had gone after his crucifixion, but that he actually arose from the realm of the dead.

In view of the emphasis which was apparently laid by the author of R not upon the significance and value, but upon the reality of the death and resurrection of Christ, it would seem that he must have had in mind the denial of their reality, and felt the need of meeting it. As a matter of fact there were many docetists in his day who believed that Christ had neither died nor risen again. Ignatius in his opposition to such docetists some decades earlier found himself obliged to lay stress upon the truth both of the death and of the resurrection. Thus in *Trall.* 9 he says: "Be ye deaf therefore when any man speaketh unto you apart from Jesus Christ, who was of the race of David, who was son of Mary, who was truly born, ate and drank, was truly persecuted under Pontius Pilate, was truly crucified and died, in the sight of those in heaven and on earth and under the earth; who also was truly raised from the dead, his father having raised him; who in like manner will also raise us who believe on him;" and still more clearly in *Smyrn.* 2: "For he suffered all these things for our sakes; and he suffered truly, as also he raised himself truly; not as certain unbelievers say that he suffered in semblance, being themselves semblance. And according as their opinions are, so shall it happen to them, for they are without body and demon like."

Marcion, strangely enough in view of his docetism, did not question the fact of Christ's death. On the contrary he followed Paul in accepting it, as also the resurrection of Christ and his subsequent appearances to his disciples (cf. Tertullian, *Adv. Marc.*, I. 11; II. 27, 28; III. 11, 19, 23; IV. 41 seq.) At the same time his docetism was such that it was felt by his opponents, or at any rate by Tertullian, that he could not truly believe in the death and resurrection, that he could not look upon either event as actually real.
And so Tertullian frequently represents Marcion as holding that Christ died and rose again only in appearance, and he thinks it necessary to insist over against him upon the reality not only of Christ's birth and of his human flesh, but also of his death and resurrection (cf. *Adv. Marc.*, II. 27; III. 8, 11, 19; IV. 21, 42, 43; V. 5, 7, 20; and *De Carne Christi*, 5). It is possible that the same consideration led the author of R to assert that Christ Jesus, the son of the creator and ruler of the universe (cf. Tertullian, *Adv. Marc.* III. 19, 23), was crucified and buried and rose again. Or it may be that it was popularly supposed, or taken for granted at the time R was written, that Marcion denied the death and resurrection of Christ altogether, as so many docetists were doing; and it

may be that the author of R shared the supposition, for there is no reason to believe that he had read the *Antitheses*, as Tertullian had. The symbol in this as in other parts was probably framed, not in the light of a careful study of Marcion's system, but only under the influence of the popular conception of his views. In any case, whether or not the author was aware, as Tertullian was, of Marcion's inconsistent acceptance of the death and resurrection, the assertion that Christ was crucified and buried and rose again, was most natural, indeed we may fairly say indispensable in an anti-Marcionitic creed.

Ἀναβάντα εἰς τοὺς οὐρανούς.

References to the ascension are not so common in early Christian literature as to justify the expectation that it must inevitably be mentioned in a Christian creed of the second century. The exaltation of Christ to the right hand of God formed an important part of the earliest Christian tradition, and of course the exaltation presupposes the ascension, but the special mention of the latter is rare. It is possible that in the original form of the gospel tradition the ascension was not reported at all, and that a final departure of Christ from his disciples, such as is recorded in Acts I. 9, was marked off from his many sudden departures only after reflection upon his exaltation and second coming (cf. my *Apostolic Age*, p. 39).

The ascension is referred to rarely in the New Testament (in Mark XVI. 19, Acts I. 2, 9, and in some manuscripts of Luke XXIV. 51; cf. also John VI. 62, XX. 17; Eph. IV. 8; I. Tim. III. 16), only once in the Apostolic fathers (Barnabas 15), once in Aristides (*Apol.*, 2), and a number of times in Justin (*Apol.*, I. 26, 31, 42, 45, 46, 50, 51, 54; *Dial.*, 17, 32, 34, 36, 38, 39, 68, 82, 85, 132). While the ascension is thus mentioned frequently in Justin, the four items which occur in R (Resurrection, Ascension, Session, and Second coming) are not once found together in Justin, or in any other writer prior to R. Resurrection, ascension and session are found in Justin, *Dial.*, 36 (cf. also *Apol.*, 42 and 45); resurrection, ascension, and second coming in Justin, *Dial.*, 136; resurrection and ascension in Barnabas 15, Aristides 2, and Justin, *Apol.*, 31, 46, 50; *Dial.*, 17, 32, 68, 82, 85; ascension and second coming in Justin, *Dial.*, 34.

It is worth noticing in this connection, as indicating how slowly the tradition of the ascension became fixed, that the word for ascension varies greatly in the passages where the fact is referred to (ἀναλαμβάνω, ἀναφέρω, ἐπαίρω, ἀγάγω, ἀνίημι, ἀναβαίνω in Barnabas and three times in Justin, and oftenest of all in Justin ἀνέρχομαι), and that there was no certainty in the second century as to the length of time that had elapsed between the resurrection and ascension, some placing the ascension on the day of the resurrection (Barnabas 15), some forty days later (Acts I. 9), some many months and even ten years later (the Valentinians, Ophites and other Gnostics, see Harnack in Hahn, p. 382).

In view of the facts referred to we may conclude that the mention of the ascension in R, while conceivably due to a mere desire to state in detail the most important events in Christ's career, was more probably the result of some special interest, and that interest was very likely identical with that which controlled the earlier part of the creed; for, taken in connection with the crucifixion, burial, and resurrection, the reference to the ascension, which doubtless implies a literal, visible phenomenon as in Acts I. 9, may well have been due to the Marcionitic view that the Christ Jesus who ascended to heaven was a mere spiritual being without a real human body. It also serves, whether the author intended it or not, to make it impossible to interpret "crucified and buried" as referring only to the man Jesus as distinguished from the spiritual æon Christ, which was supposed by many docetists to have ascended to heaven directly from the cross, leaving the man Jesus to die and be buried.

Καθήμενον ἐν δεξιᾷ τοῦ πατρός.

Christ's session at the right hand of God is

referred to very frequently in the New Testament, and a few times in post-canonical literature prior to R (e. g., in 1 Clement 36 ; Polycarp 2; Justin, *Apol.*, 45, and *Dial.*, 32, 36. Compare also *Apol.*, 42, where it is said " Our Jesus Christ, being crucified and dead, rose again, and having ascended to heaven, reigned "). The phrase commonly used is ἐν δεξιᾷ (or ἐκ δεξιῶν as in Psalm 110) τοῦ θεοῦ (in Matthew XXVI. 64 and parallels δυνάμεως). The words of R, ἐν δεξιᾷ τοῦ πατρός, occur nowhere else in Christian literature prior to R, except in Justin, *Dial.*, 36. The phrase, which came from Psalm 110 (cf. Acts II. 33 seq.; Heb. I. 13; Justin, *Dial.*, 36 ; Tertullian, *Adv. Marc.* IV. 41, 42) was used to express the glory and especially the power of the exalted Christ. His victory over his enemies, the demons, is the fact which Justin emphasizes in *Apol.* 45, *Dial.* 32 and 36.

While the Session is not mentioned frequently in early Christian literature outside of the New Testament its repeated occurrence there would make its insertion in a Christian creed of the second century quite natural, whether the desire was simply to state the most important events in Christ's career, or to emphasize his exaltation and dignity and power over against heathen and unbelievers. At the same time, it too is entirely in place in an anti-Marcionitic creed and has special significance in such a creed. It is not to be taken by itself, but in connection with the article on the judgment which immediately follows, and for which it prepares the way. It is not simply that Christ ascended into heaven and will come *thence* to judge men, but that he is at the right hand of the Father — the same God referred to in the first article — at once father of the universe and father of Christ (the words τοῦ πατρός here having a definiteness of meaning that τοῦ θεοῦ would lack), and that it is from his right hand, that is with his commission and by his authority, that he will come as judge. The reference to the Session thus makes the matter much more definite than it would otherwise be and prevents any quibbling on the part of Marcion and his followers touching the relation between Christ and the creator and ruler of the universe after the close of Christ's earthly career, as the first and second article made impossible any doubt touching his origin.

The use of an expression taken from the Old Testament is also significant, for it emphasizes again, in passing, the identity between the God of the Old Testament — the creator and ruler of the world — and the Father of Jesus Christ.

Ὅθεν ἔρχεται κρῖναι ζῶντας καὶ νεκρούς.

The article on the judgment is found in this exact form nowhere else before Irenæus, though we have language very closely approaching it (see above, p. 98). The phrase ζῶντες καὶ νεκροί occurs frequently in early Christian literature in connection with the judgment: for instance in Acts X. 42; 2 Tim. IV. 1; 1 Peter IV. 5; 2 Clement 1; Barnabas 7; Polycarp 2; Justin, *Dial.*, 118.

The belief that Christ would come again to judge the world was very common in the church from an early day (cf., e. g., Matt. XXV. 31 seq., 2 Tim. IV. 1, Jude 14, Barnabas 15, Polycarp 2, Justin, *Dial.*, 31, 36, 49, 132). Christ is spoken of as judge, without any explicit reference to his second coming, which however may be regarded as always assumed, in many other passages, thus in John V. 22 seq., Acts X. 42, XVII. 31, Rom. II. 16, Barnabas 5, 7, Polycarp 6, 2 Clement 1, Justin, *Apol.* 53, *Dial.*, 46, 47, 58, 118. On the other hand, God is spoken of as judge in a number of passages, for instance in Rom. III. 6; 1 Peter I. 17, IV. 5; Justin, *Dial.*, 141. The two conceptions are not inconsistent, for Christ was thought of as the agent of God in executing judgment, and so the judgment might be spoken of indifferently as God's or Christ's. Compare Acts XVII. 31, Rom. II. 16, and Justin, *Dial.* 58 ("the judgment which God the maker of all things shall hold through my Lord Jesus Christ"), where the relation between God and Christ in the act of judging is brought out very clearly.

Other purposes than the judgment are often connected with the second coming of Christ in early Christian literature: thus for example Christ comes to save (1 Thess. I. 10, 2 Clement 17); to save and condemn (Justin, *Apol.*, 52; *Dial.*, 35, 45, 121); to reward men according to their works (Matt. XVI. 27; Barnabas 21); to condemn the wicked (2 Thess. I. 7; Justin, *Dial.*, 39); to receive or establish a kingdom (2 Clement 17; Justin, *Dial.*, 39). The second coming is also spoken of frequently without any indication of its purpose, for instance in Matt. XXIV. 30, XXVI. 64 and parallels; Mark VIII. 38; Acts I. 11; 1 Cor. XV. 23; 1 Thess. II. 19, III. 13, IV. 15 seq., V. 23; 2 Thess. II. 1, 8; Jas. V. 7; 2 Peter III. 4; 1 John II. 28; *Didache*, 16; Justin, *Apol.*, 51; *Dial.*, 14, 34, 54, 83, etc. It is evident therefore that the allusion to the judgment in the present article is intentional, and that we are not to interpret it simply as part of a traditional formula relating to the parousia. It is not that the author refers simply to Christ's second coming, but that he refers to the coming for judgment, the purpose being indicated as well as the act itself. This is a very significant fact, for in no other article of the creed is there a reference to purpose of any kind. Why then have we such a reference here? It might be thought that the practical importance of the belief in a judgment led to its inclusion. It is true that the judgment is made much of by nearly all early Christian writers, but why should this single practical truth be mentioned in R and no other? Why is there no reference to faith, to love, to good works, to conduct of any kind, to the law of Christ, to salvation by him, to heaven and hell? Evidently the author of the creed was not concerned with practical truths as such, and it is impossible, unless we attribute to him a degree of carelessness and looseness of thought which the structure of the creed as a whole by no means justifies, to suppose that this single article was inserted with a practical purpose.

Again it might be suggested that the author refers to the judgment simply to increase the emphasis upon the majesty and authority of Christ over against heathen and unbelievers. Not that he is interested in the judgment as such, but in the fact that Christ is judge. This is a possible explanation, but if this were the author's design he might fairly have been expected to add a reference to the glory in which Christ should return, or to the fact that he was to rule the world. References of this kind are very numerous both within and without the New Testament in connection with the second coming, and especially the fact that he was to come as a king, and reign over all, would have met the author's purpose capitally.

On the other hand, if the creed was anti-Marcionitic in interest and purpose, there was the best reason in the world for the insertion of an article on the judgment and in exactly the form which we have in R. Marcion, as we learn from many passages in Tertullian's work against him (*Adv. Marc.*, I. 26, 27; IV. 8, 15, 17, 19, 21, 23, 24, 29, 35 seq.; V. 4, 7, 8, 13, 16), denied that Jesus Christ, or his Father — a God of pure love and mercy — would execute judgment. And Tertullian regards the denial as so serious that he argues the question at great length. It is evident from his attitude in the matter that an article upon the judgment could not well be wanting in an anti-Marcionitic creed. The article in R with its assertion not simply that there will be a judgment, but that Christ Jesus, who is now at the right hand of the Father, will come from thence, that is with the Father's authority and as his agent, to judge all men, repudiates the position of Marcion in the most definite and thoroughgoing way.

Καὶ εἰς πνεῦμα ἅγιον.

Πνεῦμα ἅγιον is the reading of the *Psalterium Æthelstani* and is to be preferred to Marcellus' τὸ ἅγιον πνεῦμα, because in all the Latin texts of R we have the order *Spiritum Sanctum* (see above, p. 43). In the New Testament and early Christian literature the form varies between πνεῦμα ἅγιον, τὸ πνεῦμα τὸ ἅγιον, and τὸ ἅγιον πνεῦμα. The first is most common, the third least so, but the three are used indifferently by the same writers, without any distinction of meaning. In the baptismal formula of Matthew and the *Didache*, and in the benediction of 2 Cor. XIII. 13, we have τὸ ἅγιον πνεῦμα, but in the baptismal formula of Justin Martyr (*Apol.*, 61) πνεῦμα ἅγιον occurs.

The Spirit was called ἅγιον to indicate its connection with God, and to distinguish it from human and other spirits. The word does not signify primarily pure or holy in an ethical sense, but reverend or worthy of veneration and so belonging to God, divine, heavenly. The Holy Spirit was referred to in early Christian literature, with no suggestion of a difference in meaning, as πνεῦμα ἅγιον, πνεῦμα θεοῦ, πνεῦμα προφητικόν, etc., or πνεῦμα alone. Compare for instance the three parallel passages: Matt. III. 16 (πνεῦμα θεοῦ), Mark I. 10 (τὸ πνεῦμα), and Luke III. 22 (τὸ πνεῦμα τὸ ἅγιον). In the Epistle of Barnabas, though the Spirit is referred to four times, the phrase "Holy Spirit" does not occur. In the epistles of Paul it occurs twelve times out of some ninety references to the Spirit; in the remainder of the New Testament frequently; in 1 Clement eight times out of ten; in Ignatius three times out of ten; in the *Didache* twice out of seven times; in the Martyrdom of Polycarp three times, in Hermas and Justin very often. That we have in R the phrase πνεῦμα ἅγιον instead of πνεῦμα alone, or πνεῦμα θεοῦ, or some similar phrase, is doubtless due simply to the fact that that particular phrase was in the baptismal formula upon which R was based. The author of R was evidently interested not to make any special statements about the Spirit or to emphasize his character and nature, but merely to reproduce the reference in the formula, and if the latter had said πνεῦμα θεοῦ, or πνεῦμα Χριστοῦ, or πνεῦμα προφητικόν, or πνεῦμα alone, we should doubtless have had the same expression in R.

The lack of qualifying phrases and of references to character, nature, and activity in connection with the article on the Spirit is very significant. It is evident that there was no special reason for the mention of the Spirit in R, as there was for the mention of God and of Christ, beyond the fact that it had a place in the baptismal formula upon which the creed was based. (Upon the reason for the reference to the Spirit in the baptismal formula, see below, p. 183). But this fact throws light upon the purpose of the creed as a whole. If its purpose had been to give general expression to the faith of the church, or to expound the baptismal formula in all its parts, more must have been said concerning the Holy Spirit. It is true that there was some uncertainty as to the nature of the Spirit and his relation to God and Christ, but his activity was universally recognized, and the literature of the period shows that the Christians of the day had enough to say on the subject. The only reasonable explanation of the silence of R is that the author was concerned to state the common faith of the church only in so far as it had been impugned, and as there was no heresy abroad touching the Holy Spirit — as every Christian believed in him — it was unnecessary to say anything upon the subject. Had the creed not been based upon the baptismal formula probably the Spirit would not have been mentioned at all. As it was, the formula was reproduced, but expounded only in so far as the spread of false teaching made necessary.

The conception of the Holy Spirit was received by the Christians from the Jews. It originated among the latter and was one of the consequences of the effort to find some means of communication between the transcendent God and the universe. The distance and separation of God from the world were increasingly emphasized by post-exilic Judaism, and the emphasis led to the need of intermediate beings or forces or principles. At the time of Christ the conception of the Holy Spirit, which was not thought of as an independent personality, but as the power of God working especially in inspiration and salvation, was the general possession of the Jews, and whenever the divine activity, inspiring and saving men, was thought of, it was common to use the term Holy Spirit or Spirit of God. And so the prophecy of Joel, that in the last times God would pour out of his Spirit upon all flesh, meant that the enlightening and saving influence of God would be felt as it had not been before. The conception of the Spirit passed over into the Christian church, and it was believed by all Christians, whether they shared the Jewish conception of the divine transcendence or not, that the Spirit was now especially active; that the age in which they lived, the age which the prophets had foretold, was the age of the Spirit in an especial degree, which meant simply that it was an age of peculiar and immediate divine activity, inspiring, enlightening, blessing, saving. The early Christians did not speculate touching the nature of the Spirit and his relation to God and to Christ, but when they spoke of the Spirit they meant commonly, not a special person or hypostasis, but the divine power working in the world, or among men, or especially within the Christian church, the peculiar sphere of his activity. Paul frequently uses the terms God, Christ, and Spirit interchangeably. Evidently the term Spirit meant to him the spiritual nature of God, which could be separated from God of course only in thought. In that spiritual nature Christ also shared, and so he too could be spoken of as Spirit.

Most of the early Christian writers who refer to the Spirit leave us quite in the dark as to their conception of his relation to God and to Christ. Hermas of Rome is the first of the fathers to attempt to define the matter, and he represents the Spirit as the son of God (*S.*, IX. 1), and says that God "made the Holy pre-existent Spirit, which created the whole creation, to dwell in flesh which he desired" (*S.*, V. 6); so that Christ was thought of by him as a man in whom the Spirit of God dwelt, setting him apart from and raising him above all other men, and making him Saviour and Lord.

The Holy Spirit among the Jews represented an interest somewhat similar to that which led to the Logos conception among the Greeks; and in Justin Martyr, who made large use of the Logos conception, we find considerable confusion as to the relation between the Logos and the Holy Spirit. Justin distinctly says that the Logos, or Son of God, and the Spirit are the same (*Apol.*, 33; so also Theophilus, II. 10; and compare Justin, *Apol.*, 36, where the Logos is represented as inspiring the prophets, a function commonly ascribed to the Spirit, e. g., ibid., 38, 39, etc.); and yet under the influence of Christian tradition, which spoke of God and Christ and the Holy Spirit, as for instance in the baptismal formula, Justin found it necessary to distinguish between Christ and the Holy Spirit, and as the former was the Son of God, and so the incarnate Logos, he had to distinguish between the Spirit and the Logos; but what the distinction was he could not say and the result was serious confusion. Had it not been for the threefold baptismal formula, the church would possibly have contented itself with a duality: God the Father and the Logos, or Spirit, or Son of God, who became incarnate in Christ. It is significant that in R we have neither the dual conception, which identifies the Spirit with the Son of God incarnate in Christ, nor the trinal conception, which distinguishes the two and makes two divine hypostases in addition to God the Father. What we have in R is simply God, and his Son, the historic Christ, and the Holy Spirit, without any hint of the relation between the Spirit and God or Christ, without any hint that the author had thought at all about that relationship, though it was engaging the attention of at least some of his contemporaries in Rome. That he simply reproduces the baptismal formula without any suggestion of the problem involved is certainly, under existing circumstances, strong evidence of the exclusively anti-heretical or anti-Marcionitic character of the creed. So far, then, as the Old Roman Symbol goes, a Christian who accepted it might hold any opinion he chose, or might have no opinion, touching the relation of the Spirit to God or to Jesus Christ.

Ἁγίαν ἐκκλησίαν.

As shown above, p. 92 seq., these words very likely formed no part of the original text of R, but were added some time before the middle of the third century. The phrase is not found in the New Testament, though we have in Eph. V. 27 the words "that he may present it to himself a glorious church, not having spot or wrinkle or any such thing, but that it may be holy and without blemish (ἁγία καὶ ἄμωμος)," and in 1 Peter II. 5 Christians are spoken of as "a holy priesthood" (ἱεράτευμα ἅγιον), and in II. 9 as "a holy nation" (ἔθνος ἅγιον). The phrase occurs in the writings of the first and second centuries only in Hermas, *Vis.*, I. 1, 3; in Ignatius, *Trall.*, inscr.; in the *Martyrdom of Polycarp*, inscr. (τῆς ἁγίας καὶ καθολικῆς ἐκκλησίας); in Theophilus II. 14; in Apollonius, according to Eusebius, *H. E.*, V. 18; and in Clement of Alexandria, *Strom.* VII. 14 (see Kattenbusch, II. p. 703 seq.). We have also λαὸς ἅγιος used of the Christians in Barnabas 14 and Justin, *Dial.*, 119; and in the *Didache*, chap. 10, the church is spoken of as sanctified (τὴν ἁγιασθεῖσαν εἰς τὴν σὴν βασιλείαν).

Though the phrase ἁγία ἐκκλησία is so rare in early Christian literature, its meaning, if it formed a part of the original text of R, can hardly be doubtful. The adjective ἅγιος whether used with persons or things, meant properly not *pure* but *sacred*, that is, *set apart for* or *belonging to God*.[1] And the phrase ἁγία ἐκκλησία in the first or early second century would naturally express, not the ethical purity or sinlessness of the church or of Christians, but the belief that the church was an institution founded by and belonging to God, not man. This conception of the Christian church was common among Christians from an early day. The church was thought of not as a mere voluntary association of disciples of Christ, but as a divine institution established and sustained by God, an institution composed of men and women called and set apart by God to be his own elect people. The conception that Christian believers were called and set apart by God was very natural on Jewish ground. For sharing as the early Jewish disciples did in the ancestral consciousness of belonging to God's covenant people, they could hardly do otherwise than see in themselves, and in those who should become associated with them as followers of Jesus the Messiah, the real kernel of the Jewish race and the true object of God's covenant (cf. Acts II.

---

[1] It is in this sense that the early Christians were commonly called ἅγιοι, not as sinless, but as called and set apart by God. Compare for instance Hermas, *Vis.*, I. 1, II. 2, III. 8, where the sins of the ἅγιοι are spoken of.

39, III. 25). But there is no hint in our sources and it is altogether unlikely that they thought of themselves as constituting a new people, or that they called themselves a church as distinguished from their unbelieving countrymen, and separated themselves even in thought from the household of faith to which they belonged by birth. But when Christianity passed the boundaries of the Jewish people and made a home for itself on Gentile soil, and when new Christian communities grew up divorced entirely from Judaism, the basis was given for the idea that the Christian family constituted the true Israel of God, a new covenant people taking the place of the old and inheriting all the privileges which the Jews by their rejection of Christ had forfeited. Compare for instance I Clement 29, 30, 59, 64; 2 Clement 2; Barnabas 6, 13, 14; Justin, *Dial.*, 11, 24, 26, 110, 116, 118 seq., 130, etc. According to Hermas the church was created before all things, and even the world was framed for its sake (*Vis.*, II. 4); and a similar belief is expressed by his contemporary the author of 2 Clement (chap. 14).

If R was intended to be a general statement of the faith of Christians at the time it was framed, there would be nothing strange in the insertion of the article on the church, but the character and general purpose of the creed being what they are it is difficult to understand the presence of the article. It might possibly be explained as a protest against the Gnostic and Marcionitic denial of the holiness of the church at large, and their assertion that only a select few within the church were elected to salvation, but it is too general in its form to lend itself easily to such an interpretation.

On the other hand, as will be shown a little later, there are the best of reasons for the insertion of such an article in the early part of the third century, the period to which external testimony would lead us to assign it. In the meantime let us examine the next article, which is closely connected with the article on the church and throws light back upon its interpretation.

Ἄφεσιν ἁμαρτιῶν.

External testimony is against the presence of this article in the original text of R (see p. 94). Does the internal evidence confirm or contradict the external? And, first, was there reason for the insertion of such an article at the time the creed was framed?

We have already seen that it is impossible to explain the creed satisfactorily as a general summary of the faith of the church, or as an enumeration of the blessings of Christianity. Opposition to false teaching alone accounts adequately for the portion which we have already studied. It is unlikely therefore that the present article was added without any polemic reference, simply as a positive statement of one of the blessings of Christianity. But even if this consideration, drawn from the nature of the creed as a whole, were waived, and it were assumed that one of the purposes of the creed was to enumerate the blessings of Christianity, an examination of the literature of the period shows that forgiveness of sins was not a blessing which we might expect to find mentioned. It is true that the forgiveness of sins constituted an important element in the gospel of Christ; that his emphasis was upon the love rather than the severity of God; that he preached God rather as a father than a judge. But what was true of Christ was not true of the church of the second century.

The phrase ἄφεσις ἁμαρτιῶν is very rare in early Christian literature. Outside of the New Testament, where it occurs about a dozen times, it is found before Irenæus only in Barnabas (six times), in Justin Martyr (the same number of times), and in Hermas (only once, *M.*, IV. 3, 3). But it is not simply that the phrase is rare; the idea of the forgiveness of sins is very little emphasized in the literature of the second century. There is only one reference to forgiveness in Ignatius (*Phil.* 8), only one in the *Didache* (XI.), and none in Polycarp and 2 Clement. While the love of God is occasionally referred to it is as lawgiver and judge that the early Christians chiefly think of him, and the forgiveness of sins is not commonly represented as one of the blessings that distinguish Christianity from other religions. On the contrary, it is the ethical rigor of Christianity that is chiefly emphasized. The Christian is judged more severely than other men, not less so. The man who becomes a Christian assumes ethical responsibilities which he did not have before, and if he does not live as he should he can hope only for condemnation, not forgiveness. Compare for instance Hermas, *Vis.*, II. 2; *M.*, IV. 1; *Sim.* V. 7; 2 Clement 6 seq; Aristides, *Apol.*, 17. Ecclesiastical discipline was accordingly very strict. Serious offenders were excommunicated, and once excommunicated they could not ordinarily be received back again into communion. Compare Heb. VI. 4 seq., X. 26 seq.; Hermas, *M.*, IV. 3. It is true that there was general agreement among Christians that repentance and baptism effected the remission of a man's prebaptismal sins, and enabled him to start upon the Christian life with a clean record, but thenceforth it was judgment, not forgiveness, which the Christian was to look for, and it was the thought of the divine severity, not the divine mercy, which was to control his life. And so the unqualified phrase ἄφεσις ἁμαρτιῶν does not express the faith of the church of the early second century. One might almost say that its faith would be more accurately expressed by a denial of the forgiveness of sins than by an unqualified assertion of it!

It is thus impossible to explain the article as giving utterance to one of the important elements in the common belief of the church at the time of the composition of R. Was there then any special reason in the situation in which the author was placed when he wrote the creed that would account for its insertion? It cannot have been introduced with an anti-Marcionitic purpose, for one of the principal indictments brought against Marcion by his opponents was that he emphasized the forgiving love of God at the expense of his avenging justice. But we learn from the *Shepherd* of Hermas that the subject of the forgiveness of sins was under discussion at about the time R was composed, the question as to whether there is forgiveness for post-baptismal sins being apparently a burning question then in Rome (cf. *M.*, IV.). It might be thought that it was this discussion which led to the addition of the article. But in the light of the writings of Hermas himself, of 2 Clement, and of Justin Martyr, all of which belong to about this period, and in the light of the controversy caused more than half a century later by the disciplinary laxity of Bishop Callixtus, it is impossible to suppose that the church of Rome committed itself at or soon after the middle of the second century to the advanced position touching post-baptismal sins which is involved in the sweeping and unconditioned phrase ἄφεσις ἁμαρτιῶν.

Is there then any other period at which such an article might naturally have been added? As already seen, the article formed a part of the creed of Cyprian and Novatian, so that it must have been added before the middle of the third century. And as a matter of fact in the early part of that century conditions existed in Rome which fully explain its introduction. One of the results of the Gnostic and Montanistic conflicts was a radical change in the conception of the church. Instead of being regarded as a community of saints, it was now thought of as an ark of salvation, an institution containing both good and evil, outside of which salvation was impossible. Whereas, therefore, the effort had formerly been to keep the church pure by excluding permanently all unworthy members, the effort now was to induce all that would to enter the church in order to make their salvation possible. Under these circumstances the old disciplinary rigor was relaxed and the church definitely adopted the principle that all post-baptismal sins may be forgiven after repentance and suitable penance. Callixtus, Bishop of Rome from 217 to 222, first publicly enunciated the new principle, in an edict in which he declared that he would pardon and receive back into the church all offenders, except murderers and apostates. (See Tertullian's *De Paenitentia* and *De Pudicitia;* and compare Preuschen: *Tertullian's Schriften De Paenitentia und De Pudicitia mit Rücksicht auf die Bussdisciplin;* Rolffs: *Indulgenzedikt des Kallistus;* and Harnack: *Dogmengeschichte,* I., p. 331 seq., English translation, II. 108 seq.) His action caused a schism in the church of Rome — Hippolytus leading the opposition — but the church sustained him, and the principle which he enunciated was ultimately made general, so as to cover all sins. This controversy in Rome supplies a sufficient motive for the insertion in the creed of the article ἄφεσις ἁμαρτιῶν. The question between the two parties was not a question of detail, as to whether more or fewer sins should be regarded as mortal sins, but a question of principle, as to whether the church is a community of saints or an ark of salvation, as to whether therefore the old disciplinary rigor should be maintained, and pardon for flagrant sins committed after baptism be refused, or the lax principle adopted of opening even to serious offenders the possibility of readmission to the church. Throughout the controversy the one party appealed to the forgiving love,[1] the other

---

[1] Such passages as Ex. XXXIV. 6, Ezek. XVIII. 23, XXIII. 11, Hos. VI. 6, Matt. XI. 19, XIII. 29, Luke VI. 36 seq., XV., Rom. XIV. 4, 2 Cor. II. 6 seq., 1 Tim. V. 10, 1 John I. 7, were appealed to

# HISTORICAL INTERPRETATION 161

to the stern justice of God, and so the addition of the general phrase ἄφεσις ἁμαρτιῶν to the creed would express in the clearest possible way the principles of the laxer party, the party of the majority, which prevailed over Hippolytus and his supporters.

In the light of what has been said we can hardly hesitate to accept the conclusion to which the external testimony also points, that ἄφεσις ἁμαρτιῶν did not constitute a part of the original text of R, but was added in the first half of the third century.[1] The interpretation of the article, if added then, is abundantly clear, as has been shown.

Our interpretation of the article on the forgiveness of sins throws light upon the article on the

by the Callixtine party. See Hippolytus, Phil. IX. 7 (12); and Tertullian, *De Paenitentia* 8, *De Pudicitia* 2, 7 seq., 9 seq., 13, 18 seq.

[1] Attention should have been called on p. 94 to the fact that the article on the remission of sins is wanting in the baptismal interrogatories of the *Canones Hippolyti* (Hahn, § 31d; cf. Kattenbusch, I. p. 320 seq.), of the newly discovered Latin translation of the *Egyptian Church Order* (see Funk in the *Theologische Quartalschrift*, 1899, p. 174 seq. and Kattenbusch, II. p. 732 seq.), and of the *Testamentum Jesu Christi* (see the *editio princeps* of Rahmani, 1899, p. 129). In all these forms μονογενῆ and τὸν κύριον ἡμῶν are also wanting; while ἁγίαν ἐκκλησίαν is lacking in the first but present in the two others, and σαρκὸς ἀνάστασιν is found only in the second. It seems altogether probable that these texts are based upon R, but as the date and place of composition of the documents containing them are very uncertain we cannot be sure of the significance of the omissions referred to, or whether they have any significance at all.

church. As already seen, external testimony is against its existence in the original text of the creed, and it is difficult to explain its purpose if it was a part of R in the beginning. But the situation in Rome in the early third century would account for the addition of an article on the church as well as on the forgiveness of sins. In the primitive period excommunicated offenders were commonly left to the mercy of God, who might forgive them if he chose, forgiveness being in the hands of God, not of the church. But the changed conception of the church, which has been referred to, involved the assumption that the church has the power to forgive sins. Compare the words of Callixtus' edict, "habet potestatem ecclesia delicta donandi" (see Tertullian: *De Pudicitia*, 21, and Rolffs, *op. cit.*, p. 114); and compare also Cyprian's "remissionem peccatorum per sanctam ecclesiam" (*Ep.* 69, 70). Moreover, the readmission of gross offenders led naturally to the accusation that the holiness or purity of the church was thus sacrificed, and that it became an unholy institution. Over against such accusations the supporters of the new conception maintained that the church is a holy institution, not because its members are holy, but because it has the means of grace, and so the power of promoting their holiness and saving them (cf. Hippolytus, *Phil.*, IX. 7; Tertullian, *De Pudicitia*, 21; Cyprian,

*Ep.*, 69). And so the conjunction of the two phrases ἁγίαν ἐκκλησίαν and ἄφεσιν ἁμαρτιῶν must express, in the early part of the third century, at once the belief that there is forgiveness of sins through the church, and the belief that the church is holy even though she forgives sins. The form in which the two articles are phrased by Cyprian — *remissionem peccatorum per sanctam ecclesiam* — expresses the former belief more clearly, but lays the emphasis upon it at the expense of the latter, while the juxtaposition of the two in R emphasizes equally the holiness of the church and the forgiveness of sins, and at least suggests the connection between them, which Cyprian, because of his controversy with Novatian, was concerned to emphasize particularly.

That these two articles were inserted immediately after "Holy Spirit" and before "Resurrection of the flesh," instead of being added at the end of the creed, was due doubtless in part to the fact that they belong logically before the mention of the resurrection, and in part to the ἅγιον of the article on the Spirit, with which ἁγίαν of the article on the church naturally connected itself.[1]

[1] Confirmatory evidence of the conclusion that the articles on the remission of sins and the holy church were added to R in the early third century under the influence of the controversy touching the forgiveness of post-baptismal sins may possibly be found in the surprisingly sparing use made of R by Hippolytus and Novatian.

Σαρκὸς ἀνάστασιν.

There is no reason to doubt that this article constituted a part of the original text of R (see above, pp. 55, 85 seq.), but the testimony of Irenæus and Tertullian leaves its place in the creed, and its connection with what precedes, somewhat uncertain. Thus in Irenæus we have it connected twice with the return of Christ: *ad resuscitandam omnem carnem*. In Tertullian we have *judicare . . . per carnis etiam resurrectionem* (*Virg. Vel.*, 1); *profanos judicandos . . . facta utriusque partis resuscitatione, cum carnis resurrectione* (*De Praescriptione*, 13); *unum deum . . . et Christum Jesum . . . et carnis resurrectionem* (*De Praescriptione*, 36). But this variety was doubtless due to the fact that in the original R the article stood by itself at the close of the creed, and so could be displaced, and brought in elsewhere at will, without interfering with the general structure of the symbol.

That there should be appended to a three-membered creed, based upon the threefold baptismal formula, an article entirely unrelated to what precedes, shows the tremendous importance of the article in the eyes of the author of R. It would have been easy to work it into the section on Christ (as Irenæus and Tertullian do), and thus preserve the symmetry of the creed, and its character as an exposition of the baptismal formula, but evidently the author wished to give especial emphasis to the resurrection of the flesh, and so added it as a separate article. This must be kept in mind in our interpretation of it.

The phrase σαρκὸς ἀνάστασις is found nowhere in Christian literature before the composition of R, except in Justin's *Dialogue,* chapter 80 ; but the belief in the resurrection of the flesh was widespread from an early day. In fact the belief in a resurrection, which was practically universal, commonly, though not always, meant among the early Christians a belief in the resurrection of the flesh, that is, of the present material body. This is clearly indicated in Rev. XX. 4 seq. ; 1 Clement, 24 seq. ; 2 Clement, 9, 14 ; Hermas, *Sim.,* V. 7, 2 ; Ignatius, *Eph.* 7, *Smyrn.* 2 ; *Mart. Polyc.* 14 ; Justin Martyr, *Apol.* I. 18 seq., *Dial.* 80 ; and there can be little doubt that in many other cases where the resurrection is referred to without specification as to its character, it is a fleshly resurrection that is in mind, for that was the kind of resurrection that was believed among the Jews as a preliminary condition of entrance into the kingdom of the Messiah. (Cf. my *Apostolic Age,* p. 452 seq.) The twenty-fourth chapter of First Clement is instructive in this connection, for while Clement does not speak particularly of a resurrection of the flesh, it is clear that the very term resurrection means to him a fleshly resurrection, and that he does not think of any other kind. This is all the more significant in view of Paul's explicit denial that the flesh rises again. To Paul the resurrection is a spiritual, not a fleshly matter (cf. my *Apostolic Age*, p. 134 seq., 309 seq.), and yet to most of the early Christians the idea of a resurrection was so inseparable from the idea of the flesh that it was impossible for them to understand Paul, and his notion of the resurrection was taken to be the same as theirs. But there were some Christians, who on one ground or another denied the doctrine and accepted a spiritual resurrection only, and whether they owed their belief to Paul or not they commonly appealed to his authority in support of their position (cf. my *Apostolic Age*, p. 502). Chief among these Christians were Marcion and the Gnostics. They were dualists, and their conception of the flesh was such that its redemption seemed to them impossible, and eternal life must consist in escape from it. In this they agreed with Paul, and of course they made much of his teaching upon the subject. The result was that the nature of the resurrection became a burning question, and over against Marcion and the Gnostics, Christians began to emphasize the resurrection of the *flesh*, and to see in it one of the cornerstones of the Christian faith. And so that which was commonly implicit in the beginning became now explicit. It was not enough to assert a resurrection merely; its fleshly character must be emphasized. This insistence upon a fleshly resurrection over against the denial of it was due not only to the feeling on the part of many Christians that a future life was impossible without a resurrection of the material body (cf. Ignatius, *Smyrn.*, 2 seq.), but also to the fear that the loss of the belief in the resurrection of the present flesh for judgment would lead to immorality and impurity (cf., e. g., 2 Clement 9; Hermas, *Sim.*, V. 7. 2; Tertullian, *Adv. Marc.* V. 7). It was thus regarded as a very practical matter. The importance attaching to the belief, and the hostility of Christians to the Marcionitic and Gnostic denial of it, may be seen in Tertullian's tracts *De Carne Christi* (cf. especially chap. 1) and *De Resurrectione Carnis*, and in his work against Marcion, IV. 37; V. 7, 9 seq., 14, 18 seq.; and also in many passages in Irenæus, e. g., II. 29 seq., V. I 18, V. 2 seq., 11 seq., 31 seq. Tertullian's work against Marcion also shows how important a place the denial of the resurrection of the flesh had in Marcion's teaching (compare especially V. 19).

In the light of what has been said there can be little doubt that the article $\sigma\alpha\rho\kappa\grave{o}\varsigma$ $\dot{\alpha}\nu\acute{\alpha}\sigma\tau\alpha\sigma\iota\nu$, whose very position gives it special emphasis, was added with a distinctly polemic purpose, to emphasize the resurrection particularly of the flesh, over against the current denial of it. If R read simply ἀνάστασιν, or ἀνάστασιν νεκρῶν, or ἐκ νεκρῶν, all of which are common in the literature of the period, or even ἀνάστασιν σώματος it would be a different matter altogether. But the striking and unusual phrase σαρκὸς ἀνάστασιν, with the emphasis upon σαρκός, admits of only one explanation. Here certainly, if anywhere in the creed, the polemic interest is evident.

It is significant that nothing is said of the purpose of the resurrection and nothing of what follows it. Judgment, salvation, messianic kingdom, eternal life — the last three are not mentioned at all, and the first in another connection altogether. Nor is it said whether all men rise or only the saved.[1] Evidently it is not the purpose or consequence of the resurrection that the author is concerned to emphasize; nor does he speak of it because he wants to enumerate the blessings of Christianity, for not resurrection, which might be shared by bad as well as good, but eternal life, which was the privilege of the saved alone, was the great blessing brought by Christ (cf. John, 1 Timothy, Jude, *Didache*, 2 Clement, Hermas, Ignatius, passim). Clearly the

[1] In John, Acts, Revelation, 2 Clement, Justin Martyr, Tatian, and Athenagoras, the resurrection of the bad as well as the good is explicitly mentioned. In other cases, before Irenæus, only the resurrection of the good (as in Paul and Ignatius), or resurrection in general without specification of good or bad, is referred to.

author was interested only to repudiate the heretical and dangerous assertion that the *flesh* rises not.

The original interest of the creed in the resurrection of the flesh, as distinguished from the fact of resurrection in general, is somewhat obscured in our English version, which dates from the time of Henry VIII. It is probable that the phrase " resurrection of the body " was intended to mean the same thing as resurrection of the flesh, but in view of Paul's use of the phrase " spiritual body," the word " body " is less explicit than the word " flesh," and so the original emphasis is in part lost. The English phrase makes it possible to interpret the article in the Pauline sense, while the Greek σαρκὸς ἀνάστασιν and the Latin *carnis resurrectionem* are distinctly, though not of course intentionally, anti-Pauline.[1]

---

[1] In the *Institution of a Christian Man*, commonly known as the Bishops' Book, which was published in 1537, the article on the resurrection is given in the following enlarged form: " I believe that at doomsday all the people of the world that ever was or ever shall be unto that day shall then arise in the selfsame flesh and body which they had while they lived on earth " (see the volume entitled *Formularies of the Faith put forth by authority during the reign of Henry VIII.*, Oxford, 1825; p. 29). In *A Necessary Doctrine and Erudition for any Christian Man*, commonly known as the King's Book, and published in 1543, the article reads simply, " the resurrection of the body " (*ibid.* p. 226), so far as I am aware, its first appearance in this form. In the second prayer book of Edward VI. (1552), where the Apostles' Creed was first printed in full in the order for morning prayer the article reads in the same way, " the resurrection of the body," and this form now appears both in the order for morning and evening prayers and in the cate-

On the early Christian belief in the resurrection of the flesh, see Haller: *Lehre von der Auferstehung des Fleisches bis auf Tertullian; Zeitschrift für Theologie und Kirche*, 1892, p. 274 seq.

Looking back over the several articles of the original text of R we see that practically the whole symbol may be interpreted as anti-Marcionitic in its purpose, and that parts of it can be satisfactorily interpreted in no other way. The only words which cannot be thus explained are $\pi\nu\epsilon\hat{u}\mu a$ $\ddot{a}\gamma\iota o\nu$. But these words constituted a part of the baptismal formula upon which the symbol was based and so could not well be omitted. The very fact that no qualifying or descriptive phrases are added goes to confirm the anti-heretical interest of the creed as a whole, for it shows that where there was no heresy — as there was none in reference to the Spirit — the need was not felt of adding anything to the baptismal formula.

On the other hand not only can the whole creed be explained as inspired by hostility to the views

---

chism, and has passed into common use among English-speaking Christians. In the order for baptism, on the other hand, the English prayer book retains the original form, "the resurrection of the flesh," while the American edition simply refers to the creed without quoting it.

In Oriental symbols, $\dot{a}\nu\acute{a}\sigma\tau a\sigma\iota\nu$ $\nu\epsilon\kappa\rho\hat{\omega}\nu$, "resurrection of the dead," as in the Nicæno-Constantinopolitan creed, is common, but $\sigma a\rho\kappa\grave{o}s$ $\dot{a}\nu\acute{a}\sigma\tau a\sigma\iota\nu$ is found in the symbols of Cyril of Jerusalem, of the Apostolic Constitutions, and of Laodicea (Hahn, §§ 124, 129, 131; cf. also §§ 140 and 141).

of Marcion, there is nothing lacking which an anti-Marcionitic symbol must necessarily contain. The only important Marcionitic tenet which is not directly met in R is the rejection of the Old Testament. It would seem as if a declaration of belief in the Old Testament might have been inserted, either explicitly, or by means of a reference to the fulfilment of prophecy by Christ. But a perusal of Tertullian's work against Marcion shows that it was not the repudiation of the Old Testament in itself that was the serious thing in the eyes of Marcion's opponents, but the separation thus brought about between Christ and the creator and ruler of the universe. And so R, with its emphasis upon the fact that Christ is the son of $\theta\epsilon\grave{o}s$ $\pi\alpha\tau\acute{\eta}\rho$ $\pi\alpha\nu\tau o\kappa\rho\acute{a}\tau\omega\rho$, is true to the real interest of Marcion's opponents, even without mentioning the Old Testament. It should be noticed too that in the reference to the birth from a virgin, and especially to the session at the right hand of the Father, there is clearly implied the acceptance of Old Testament prophecy, for both of these events were prominent among the messianic prophecies in current use at that time.

Of course R might have been made much more elaborate, and some of the tenets of Marcion might have been met in more explicit terms. But the creed was intended for use as a baptismal symbol, and therefore was necessarily made simple, brief, and compact, that it might be easily learned and repeated, and was naturally phrased in positive not negative form. It is difficult to see how Marcion's positions, so far as they were of practical, not merely speculative, interest, could have been more effectively repudiated in such a baptismal symbol than they actually are. Kattenbusch says that R " ist nicht antithetisch gedacht, sondern lediglich thetisch " (II. p. 327). If he means by this only that R is phrased in positive not negative form, of course he is right. But if he means, as he evidently does, that R was constructed without any regard to heresy, it is another matter altogether. He continues " Weder die Einheit Gottes, noch seine Schöpferstellung werden betont, so unzweifelhaft sie in ihm mitgedacht und, wenn man den ersten Artikel unbefangen überlegt, auch ausgedrückt." Why emphasis upon the unity of God, and upon creation, should make R any more truly "antithetisch" than it is now it is difficult to see. A symbol directed against Gnosticism would naturally have borne a more theological character than R has, but Marcionism was a practical not a speculative system, and is fully met by the simple but pregnant statements of R.[1]

[1] Harnack is quite right in saying that R is too simple and untheological to have been framed in opposition to the Gnostics (*Chronologie der altchristlichen Litteratur*, vol. I. p. 529), but he seems

In a *regula fidei*, moreover, designed as a standard and test of orthodoxy, something else, both in form and content, might perhaps have been expected, but I am not maintaining that R was framed as a *regula fidei*. I hold that it was originally intended as a baptismal symbol pure and simple. The only question is whether the impulse which led to its composition was or was not due to the prevalence of error — to the conviction that it was important to impress upon candidates for baptism particularly those facts and truths which were most widely doubted or denied within circles that called themselves Christian. Those who think not must answer the following questions:

First, why are so many things omitted in the original text of R which constituted an essential part of the faith of the church of the first and second centuries, while other things are mentioned which are less important in themselves and bulk far less largely in the Christian literature of the period? Secondly, how does it happen that all the views of Marcion which were most offensive to the church at large are ruled out by R? And thirdly, what was it that made such a baptismal symbol necessary in the second century when the church up to that time had got on without any-

not to have considered the possibility of its having been directed against Marcion. As a matter of fact Marcionism was a very different thing from Gnosticism, and R fills all the requirements of an anti-Marcionitic baptismal confession.

thing of the kind? Most scholars that have dealt with the Apostles' creed have evidently quite failed to realize the gravity of this last question. It was no light thing for a church to adopt a baptismal symbol when nothing of the kind had existed before. Why should it suddenly find the formula of baptism which had answered for some generations insufficient? It would seem that the composition of R is just such an event as needs a crisis like that which Marcion precipitated to explain it. That Kattenbusch and others, who put the composition of R as early as the beginning of the second century, or even earlier, should take the position they do is not perhaps surprising, but that Harnack, who recognizes so clearly the significance of the crisis in the middle of the second century, and who puts the composition of R as late as 140 or 150, should still maintain that R was not called forth by false teaching of any kind is very strange.

## VI.

### THE OLD ROMAN SYMBOL AND THE BAPTISMAL FORMULA.

CHRISTIAN baptism was an outgrowth of the baptism practised by John the Baptist. John's baptism was simply a symbolic ceremony suggested undoubtedly by the various baptisms or rites of purification which were prevalent among the Jews, and was employed with the purpose of impressing vividly upon his hearers the need of that purification of life which he was preaching and of committing them by their own voluntary act to the effort to make the desired amendment. We have no record in the synoptic gospels that Jesus himself ever baptized, or that baptism was performed during his lifetime by his disciples. But it is distinctly stated in John IV. 2 that though Jesus himself did not baptize, his disciples did, and the naturalness of the rite in the light of John's baptism, and its general prevalence in the apostolic church confirm the report and make it practically certain that the rite was not introduced as an innovation after Jesus' departure. But if practised during his lifetime by his disciples it is altogether probable, in view of his uniform policy touching the announcement of his Messiahship, and in view of the fact that it was long before even his own disciples believed him to be the Messiah, that baptism had the usual Johannine form, and that it was not a baptism into or in his own name; that it was in fact simply a continuation of the practice of John with the same purpose of impressing the need of moral and religious reformation in view of the approaching kingdom, and of committing others to such reformation.

But after the departure of Jesus conditions were changed, and if baptism was continued at all it was not unnatural that it should take on a new significance. According to Acts II. 38 seq., the converts secured on the day of Pentecost were baptized, and more than that, they were baptized into the name of Jesus Christ — the first time, so far as we know, that his name was connected with the rite. This did not mean that it ceased to be a baptism of repentance, but it did mean that the repentance to which it gave expression was based upon and due to the recognition that Jesus was the Messiah, being primarily repentance for the terrible crime committed by the Jewish people in putting Jesus to death. It was most natural that a ceremony which had come into use among Jesus' disciples during his lifetime as a symbol of repentance on the part of those who wished to prepare themselves for the coming of the kingdom, should after his death be regarded as a means of declaring one's belief in his Messiahship — the fundamental truth upon which his disciples laid all the emphasis after his departure — and should thus become a symbol not simply of repentance but of acceptance of Jesus as the Christ. And so we find that the Christian formula, "Into the name of Jesus Christ" or "of the Lord Jesus," which we first hear of in connection with Pentecost, was in common use in the time of Paul, and it is altogether probable that it was in common use from the day of Pentecost on.

It is generally supposed that Christian baptism was instituted by Christ himself after his resurrection. According to the account in Matt. XXVIII. 19, he commanded his eleven apostles, as he was upon the point of leaving them finally, to "go and make disciples of all the nations, baptizing them into the name of the Father and of the Son and of the Holy Ghost;" while according to the account in the appendix of Mark's gospel, he said to them "Go ye into all the world and preach the gospel to the whole creation. He that believeth and is baptized shall be saved, but he that disbelieveth shall be condemned." But the historic accuracy of these passages is beset with serious difficulties. Of the appendix of Mark it is unnecessary to speak. It is simply a late compilation and has no independent authority. The passage in Matthew therefore stands alone. There is no sufficient reason for questioning the authenticity of vs. 19a, "Go ye therefore, and make disciples of all the nations," for it finds confirmation in Acts I. 8 (cf. also X. 42); but of the latter part of the verse, "baptizing them into the name of the Father and of the Son and of the Holy Ghost," we cannot be so sure, as appears from the following considerations:

In the first place the reference to baptism is wanting both in the Gospel of Luke and in the first chapter of Acts, where other post-resurrection utterances of Christ are recorded. It is true that the words are found in all the manuscripts covering the conclusion of Matthew, and there is therefore no support in textual criticism for their omission. But even if it be assumed that they constituted an integral part of the Gospel, it is still uncertain whether they were uttered by Christ, for the evidence of Matthew alone unsupported by any other Gospel is inconclusive.

Still further, the command respecting baptism seems out of line with Christ's general course as indicated in the Gospels. He was concerned all the time with the spiritual and the ethical, and had very little to say about the external and formal, and laid absolutely no stress upon it. He did not commonly speak and act as if he had in mind the foundation of a visible society or church with its outward conditions of membership; and that at the end he should give to a formal rite, to which he seems to have paid no attention during his ministry, so prominent a place, making its administration a part of the permanent and constant duty of the apostles, is very surprising.

Again Paul says in 1 Cor. I. 17 that Christ sent him not to baptize but to preach the gospel — a statement not easy to understand in one who claimed so strenuously to be on an equality with the older apostles, if Christ gave baptism so prominent a place as is given it in Matt. XXVIII. 19, and laid upon the Eleven the specific injunction quoted there. It would seem, if that injunction be authentic, that baptizing must have been regarded as a very important part of every apostle's work, and it is difficult to see how Paul could speak of it so slightingly, or at any rate with such indifference.

And when we consider the baptismal formula enjoined by Christ, according to Matt. XXVIII. 19, the difficulty increases. The collocation "Father, Son, and Holy Spirit" sounds strange on Christ's lips, and suggests a conception of baptism entirely foreign to the thought of his immediate disciples, and equally foreign to the thought of Paul, whose idea of baptism seems in harmony only with the use of a single name, the name of Christ, in the formula.

There is moreover no sign that the triune formula was ever employed in the apostolic age. So far as our sources enable us to judge, baptism in the earliest days was commonly into the name of Christ without mention of God and the Holy Spirit. Thus we have "Into the name of Jesus Christ" in Acts II. 38, X. 48; "Into the name of the Lord Jesus" in Acts VIII. 16, XIX. 5; "Into Christ Jesus" in Rom. VI. 3; "Into Christ" in Gal. III. 27; "Into the name of the Lord" in *Did.* XI.; Hermas, *Vis.* III. 7, 3; "Into the death of the Lord" in the *Apostolic Constitutions*, VII. 25 (a passage based upon *Did.* XI.), and *Apostolic Canons*, 50; "Into the name of the Son of God" in Hermas, *Sim.* IX. 13, 16, 17. Compare also Col. II. 2; 1 Cor. I. 13, 15; X. 2; XII. 13; Barnabas 11. There is no reference to the triune formula in the literature of the apostolic or sub-apostolic age, except in Matt. XXVIII. 19 and in the *Didache*, chap. 7. The formula was in common use before the end of the second century, but there were many Christians even as late as the middle of the third century and some at the very end of the fourth who refused to use it and insisted on baptizing in the name of Christ alone, and their attitude is difficult to explain unless they were following an earlier custom which the church at

## THE BAPTISMAL FORMULA

large had outgrown. Compare Cyprian's *Epistle to Jubaianus* (No. 73); Pseudo-Cyprian, *De Rebaptismate*, 1, 6, 7; *Apostolic Canons*, 51, which finds it necessary to forbid the use of any but the triune formula; and Ambrose, *De Spiritu Sancto*, bk. I. chap. 3, who defends the validity of the shorter formula.

When and how the triune formula arose, if it was not enjoined by Christ under the circumstances described in Matthew, we do not know. From the simple formula "Into the name of Jesus Christ" the step is a long one to the formula "Into the name of the Father and of the Son and of the Holy Spirit." But it is possible that there was an intermediate formula in which the names of God, of Jesus Christ, and of the Holy Spirit were used. Such a formula we find employed by Paul in the familiar benediction of 2 Cor. XIII. 13 — "The grace of the Lord Jesus Christ and the love of God and the communion of the Holy Spirit be with you all" — which is not the same as "Father, Son, and Holy Spirit," though commonly treated as the same. Still more significantly we find a similar formula given twice by Justin Martyr in connection with his account of Christian baptism in his first *Apology*, chap. 61 (ἐπ' ὀνόματος γὰρ τοῦ πατρὸς τῶν ὅλων καὶ δεσπότου θεοῦ, καὶ τοῦ σωτῆρος ἡμῶν Ἰησοῦ Χριστοῦ καὶ πνεύματος ἁγίου. And later in the same chapter: τὸ τοῦ πατρὸς τῶν ὅλων καὶ δεσπότου θεοῦ ὄνομα... καὶ ἐπ' ὀνόματος δὲ Ἰησοῦ Χριστοῦ, τοῦ σταυρωθέντος ἐπὶ Ποντίου Πιλάτου, καὶ ἐπ' ὀνόματος πνεύματος ἁγίου).

The collocation "God, Jesus Christ, and the Holy Spirit" is much commoner in the literature of the late first and early second centuries than "Father, Son, and Holy Spirit" (cf. Jude 20, 21; Ignatius, *Eph.* 9; *Martyrdom of Polycarp*, 14, 22; Justin Martyr, *Apology*, I. 67), and that it was the current formula, at any rate in Rome, would seem to be indicated not only by its occurrence in Justin's *Apology*, but also by Clement's frequent and exclusive use of it in different connections (compare chap. 46: ἢ οὐχὶ ἕνα θεὸν ἔχομεν καὶ ἕνα Χριστὸν καὶ ἓν πνεῦμα τῆς χάριτος τὸ ἐκχυθὲν ἐφ' ἡμᾶς; chap. 58: ζῇ γάρ ὁ θεὸς καὶ ζῇ ὁ κύριος Ἰησοῦς Χριστὸς καὶ τὸ πνεῦμα τὸ ἅγιον κ. τ. λ. Compare also chap. 16 and 42).[1]

The rise of such a threefold formula it is not difficult to understand. The conversion of the Jews to Christianity meant only their acceptance of Jesus as the Messiah, and so their bap-

[1] Reference may also be made in this connection to the third century *Didascalia*, in which it is said that the twelve apostles being assembled in Jerusalem composed the said *Didascalia* with the purpose of guarding against heresy, and directed that Christians should worship "God Almighty and Jesus Christ and the Holy Spirit" (see *Didascalia Apostolorum Syriace*, ed. Lagarde, p. 102; Zahn in the *Neue Kirchliche Zeitschrift*, 1896, p. 23; and Funk, *Die Apostolischen Konstitutionen*, p. 61).

## THE BAPTISMAL FORMULA 183

tism into the name of Jesus Christ was a full and adequate profession of their Christian faith. The God of the Christians was their God, and no confession of their belief in him was needed. But when the gospel went to the heathen the case was different. Their acceptance of Christianity meant the acceptance of the one God of the Christians, a God commonly hitherto unknown to them. And hence it would be quite natural for the custom to grow up of having the new convert declare his belief in the Christian God, as well as in Christ, in the very act of baptism.

The mention of the name of the Holy Spirit was natural enough in connection with baptism both on Jewish and Gentile soil, for Christ's baptism was thought of from the beginning as a baptism in the Holy Spirit, whom he had promised to bestow upon his disciples after his departure. (Cf. Matt. III. 11, Mark I. 8, Luke III. 16, John I. 26, 33, Acts I. 5, XIX. 1 seq.; and compare also Acts VIII. 15 seq., IX. 17, X. 44 seq.) And so the addition of the name of the Holy Spirit, whatever the conception of the Spirit might be, would not be strange at any time. But inasmuch as we find no trace of its use in the baptismal formula either by the early Jewish Christians or by Paul, it seems likely that it first came into currency somewhat later in the gentile or world church, Paul's formula of benediction perhaps contributing to it.

There are reasons for thinking that it was upon this threefold baptismal formula ("God, Jesus Christ, and Holy Spirit") that the Old Roman Symbol was based, rather than upon the triune formula of Matthew and the *Didache*. For, in the first place, the formula was apparently in use in Rome in the time of Justin Martyr, that is just about or not long before the time that the symbol was composed. In the second place the phrase πνεῦμα ἅγιον, which occurs in R, suggests Justin's formula rather than that of Matthew and the *Didache*, for Justin reads πνεῦμα ἅγιον in his statements of the baptismal formula, while Matthew and the *Didache* both read τὸ ἅγιον πνεῦμα. In the third place the order of the words in the first and second articles of R is easier to explain if R was based on the formula of Justin than if it was based on the Matthew formula. If R were based on the latter we should expect θεὸν παντοκράτορα, a familiar phrase, to follow πατέρα in the first article, and Χριστὸν Ἰησοῦν to follow υἱόν in the second. As it is, the order in R is just what we should expect if the formula was θεὸς καὶ Ἰησοῦς Χριστός or Χριστὸς Ἰησοῦς, the elaboration of the formula being accomplished by the simple addition of the qualifying phrases. In the fourth place, and most decisive of all, the theology of R agrees with the theology of the baptismal formula of Justin, but not with that of the Matthew formula. In the latter the word "Father" looks forward to the word "Son." It is the Father of the Son into whom the convert is baptized, while in R the term "Father" is used to express, not God's relation to Christ, but his relation to the universe. It is God the author and ruler of the universe who is named in the first article, and his relation to Christ is expressed only in the second article by the phrase τὸν υἱὸν αὐτοῦ. R as it stands expounds correctly the formula of Justin — "God the father of the universe, Jesus Christ, and the Holy Spirit" — but not the formula of Matthew, "Father, Son, and Holy Spirit."

In the light of these considerations it may fairly be concluded, as it seems to me, that R was based upon the former rather than the latter formula. And the last two considerations go in turn to confirm the existence and use of the formula in question at the middle of the second century in Rome.

But that formula was finally displaced by the triune formula of Matthew, which is in line with Johannine conceptions and forms of expression, and which is perhaps due to the influence of the Johannine type of thought. At any rate, it appears before the latter part of the second century only in the Gospel of Matthew and in the *Didache,* in connection with baptism, and in other connections only in Ignatius' *Epistle to the Magnesians* (chap. 13: "That ye may prosper in all things whatsoever ye do, in flesh and spirit, faith and love, in Son and Father and in Spirit:" ἐν υἱῷ καὶ πατρὶ καὶ ἐν πνεύματι).[1] All of these writings belong to the same part of the world, and in Ignatius there are certainly, in Matthew possibly other traces of the influence of the Johannine type of thought, while the author of the *Didache* was well acquainted with the Gospel of Matthew, and very likely took the triune formula from him. The Gospel of Matthew early got into general circulation both east and west, and of course the command of Christ recorded in it would inevitably influence the baptismal formula and ultimately crowd all other forms out of use. It is an interesting fact that Irenæus and Tertullian, the first westerners in whose writings we find a reference to the baptismal formula in the Matthew form, both quote the passage in Matthew's Gospel (cf. Irenæus, III. 17, 1; Tertullian, *Adv. Prax.*, 26).

---

[1] Justin, *Apol.*, 65, may perhaps also be mentioned in this connection. In speaking there of the Eucharist he says that praise is offered τῷ πατρὶ τῶν ὅλων διὰ τοῦ ὀνόματος τοῦ υἱοῦ καὶ τοῦ πνεύματος τοῦ ἁγίου. But on the other hand, in chap. 67 he says: εὐλογοῦμεν τὸν ποιητὴν τῶν πάντων, διὰ τοῦ υἱοῦ αὐτοῦ Ἰησοῦ Χριστοῦ καὶ διὰ πνεύματος τοῦ ἁγίου.

## VII.

### THE PRESENT TEXT OF THE APOSTLES' CREED.

THE *Textus Receptus* of our present Apostles' Creed runs as follows: " Credo in Deum Patrem omnipotentem, creatorem coeli et terrae, et in Jesum Christum filium ejus unicum, dominum nostrum; qui conceptus est de Spiritu Sancto, natus ex Maria Virgine, passus sub Pontio Pilato, crucifixus, mortuus et sepultus, descendit ad inferna, tertia die resurrexit a mortuis, ascendit ad coelos, sedet ad dexteram Dei Patris omnipotentis, inde venturus est judicare vivos et mortuos. Credo in Spiritum Sanctum, sanctam ecclesiam catholicam, sanctorum communionem, remissionem peccatorum, carnis resurrectionem, vitam æternam.[1]

The additions which distinguish this creed from R are 1, *Creatorem coeli et terrae* in the first article; 2, *Conceptus est* in the article on the birth; 3, *Passus* and *mortuus* in the article on the crucifixion; 4, *Descendit ad inferna* after *sepultus*; 5, *Dei* and *omnipotentis* in the article on the session; 6, *Catholicam* in the article on the church; 7,

[1] There exist a few Greek texts of this creed (Hahn, §§ 24 b, 26, 27, 28, 30, 43), but they are all translations, more or less exact, of the Latin original. See Kattenbusch, II. p. 803 seq.

*Sanctorum communionem* after the article on the church; 8, *Vitam aeternam* at the end of the creed. Upon the interpretation of these additions see in general Kattenbusch, II. p. 874–956.

1. The phrase *creatorem coeli et terrae* probably appears first in this exact form in the completed creed (cf. Hahn, §§ 24, 25, 42, 92),[1] but phrases of similar import were much earlier. Thus we find them already in Irenæus and Tertullian (see above, p. 89), who emphasized the creative activity of God over against the Gnostics; in Augustine and other North African writers; and in most of the Eastern symbols, including the Nicene and the Nicæno-Constantinopolitan creeds. The phrase may have been coined by the author of our present text, or it may have been translated from the last named creed ($\pi o \iota \eta \tau \dot{\eta} \nu$ $o \dot{v} \rho a \nu o \hat{v}$ $\kappa a \dot{\iota}$ $\gamma \hat{\eta} s$). In any case the original anti-heretical interest which had led to the emphasis upon creation by Irenæus and Tertullian no longer existed, when the present text of the creed took shape, and the addition of the phrase was doubtless due simply to the influence of earlier formulæ. See Kattenbusch, II. p. 875 seq.

2. The addition *conceptus est* appears first in the confession of the orthodox bishops assembled at the

---

[1] Whether the texts in the *Sacramentarium Gallicanum* and *Missale Gallicanum* (Hahn, §§ 66 and 67) are earlier or later than our *Textus Receptus* is uncertain. See Kattenbusch, II. p. 774 seq.

council of Ariminum in 359 A. D. (Hahn, § 166). It appears also in a symbol of uncertain date ascribed to Bishop Damasus of Rome (Hahn, § 200); in the symbols of Faustus of Riez and Cæsarius of Arles (Hahn, §§ 61, 62); and from the sixth century on is common in Gallic forms of the creed, but is apparently confined to them (see Kattenbusch, II. p. 881). As there is reason to think that the confession of the bishops at Ariminum may have been the work of Phœbadius of Agen in Gaul (see Kattenbusch, I. p. 173 seq.), the evidence points to Gaul as the home of the phrase. It was suggested perhaps by Luke I. 31, 35, and represents probably merely the desire to make more vivid and precise the reference to the birth of Christ. There is no reason to think that heresy had anything to do with its addition to the creed. See Kattenbusch, II. p. 879 seq.

3. When the words *passus* and *mortuus* were first added to the creed is uncertain. *Passus* appears both in Spanish and Gallic formulæ (before *sub Pontio Pilato* and without *qui*, as in the present text of the creed), probably as early as the fourth century, while *mortuus* seems to have been confined to Gaul. The two words occur together, with *crucifixus* and *sepultus*, as in our present text, apparently first in Cæsarius of Arles (Hahn, § 62). Whether he is himself responsible for them we do not know, but at any rate the double addition is

doubtless to be traced back to Gaul (cf. Kattenbusch, II. p. 887 seq.). There is no sign that either word was added on account of heresy. *Passus* may have been inserted for the purpose of laying especial emphasis upon Christ's sufferings, with the same interest which led Irenæus to put it in the place of the *crucifixus* of R (see above p. 95), or it may have been added without any specific interest, under the influence of the original Nicene creed, which followed the symbol of Eusebius in mentioning, as Irenæus had done, only the passion between the birth and the resurrection.

Whatever the purpose of the addition the connection of *passus* with *sub Pontio Pilato* indicates that it was not to the life of Christ as a whole that the word was intended to refer, but only to the passion in its narrower sense — the suffering endured under Pontius Pilate; and that suffering was apparently understood not as a fact additional or preliminary to the crucifixion, death, and burial, but as a general fact including all the others, so that the article is to be paraphrased, not "suffered under Pontius Pilate, and was crucified and died and was buried" but "suffered under Pontius Pilate, that is, was crucified and died and was buried" (see Kattenbusch, II. p. 890 seq.).

So far as the word *mortuus* is concerned there was apparently no other reason for its addition than the desire for completeness of statement. It adds nothing of course to the sense, for crucifixion and burial necessarily imply death.

4. The words *Descendit ad inferna* constituted a part of the creed in use in the church of Aquileia at the beginning of the fifth century, as we learn from Rufinus' *Expositio Symboli*, chap. 18. The Aquileian creed was a slightly enlarged recension of the Old Roman Symbol, and is the earliest known recension of that symbol to contain an article on the Descent into Hades. The article occurs in no other baptismal symbol of the west before the fifth century, and in none in the east at any time. It appeared, however, nearly half a century before Rufinus wrote his *Expositio* in three conciliar formulæ of the fourth century, that of Sirmium, which was written originally in Latin but of which we have only a Greek translation (Hahn, § 163), of Nicé in Thrace (Hahn, § 164), and of Constantinople (Hahn, § 167). The three are practically identical, the last two, which date respectively from 359 and 360 A. D., being in great part translations from the Latin original of the first, which was composed by Marcus Arethusa in 359, under the influence of the Antiochian symbol and perhaps also of the baptismal symbol in use in Sirmium (cf. Kattenbusch, I. p. 260, 398). As Sirmium and Aquileia were not far apart, and the relations between them were very

close, it is quite possible that the two churches had the same baptismal symbol, namely the Old Roman Symbol slightly enlarged. The article on the Descent into Hades may have found its way into that symbol either in Aquileia or in Sirmium, or for that matter in some other place in the same part of the world. That it got into the baptismal symbol first and was taken thence into the Sirmian formula composed by Marcus Arethusa seems more probable than that it was first a part of the Sirmian formula and passed from it to the baptismal symbol, for the formula contains other items which would naturally have been incorporated into the baptismal symbol if anything was; thus, for instance, ἀποθανόντα after σταυρωθέντα; καὶ τὰ ἐκεῖσε οἰκονομήσαντα, ὃν πυλωροὶ ᾅδου ἰδόντες ἔφριξαν, in connection with the Descent into Hades; ἀναστραφέντα μετὰ τῶν μαθητῶν, both before the death and after the resurrection of Christ; τεσσαράκοντα ἡμερῶν ἀναπληρουμένων, before the ascension. On the other hand if the reference to the descent was already in the baptismal symbol in the simple form which we find in Aquileia, its incorporation and elaboration in the Sirmian formula would be very natural.

The purpose of the insertion of the article in the baptismal symbol we do not know. It may have been added simply with the desire to make the article on Christ, especially on his passion, more complete, as Harnack thinks (see his article in Herzog). But it is difficult to see in that case why other items were not introduced at the same time. Moreover, it is to be noticed that the other additions to the Old Roman Symbol in the Aquileian creed — *invisibili et impassibili* in the first article, and *hujus* with *carnis* in the article on the resurrection of the flesh — were both intended to guard against error, according to Rufinus, the one being directed against the Sabellians and the other against those who spiritualized the resurrection. It seems likely therefore that the article on the Descent into Hades was added with a similar purpose. At the same time Rufinus in this case did not know what the purpose was, so that the addition must have been made before his time and apparently to meet some temporary need, or the memory of its purpose would have survived. It was maintained by King, in his work on the Apostles' creed published in 1702, that the article was directed against the Apollinarians. If Christ was not only buried but descended into the abode of the dead, he must have had a human spirit as well as a human body, which Apollinarius denied. King's explanation is ingenious but not altogether satisfactory. If the clause had been added to the creed so recently (Apollinarius' christology did not begin to attract attention much before 360) it would seem as if

Rufinus must have known the purpose of it. But while it is difficult to suppose that the article was anti-Apollinarian in its interest, it is not impossible that it was caused by the general docetic tendency which was becoming widespread in the late third and early fourth centuries as a result of the increasing acceptance of the Logos christology. The docetism which resulted from the Logos christology was not the crass docetism of the first and second centuries, which denied the reality of Christ's fleshly body, but a subtler form of docetism which confined Christ's humanity to his fleshly body and asserted that his soul, or his rational and spiritual nature, was supplied by the Logos. This form of docetism, not yet worked out systematically, was akin to the docetism of some of the early Gnostics, and was an anticipation of the more scientific and more carefully elaborated doctrine of Apollinarius (see Harnack, *Dogmengeschichte*, II., p. 302 seq.). It may have seemed to the Christians of Aquileia or its neighborhood some generations before the time of Rufinus that the Old Roman Symbol did not sufficiently safeguard the reality of Christ's death over against this new and subtler form of docetism, and so they may have added the article in question with the purpose of emphasizing the completeness of the death. (Cf. Swete, *The Apostles' Creed*, p. 61).

But whatever the purpose which led to the addition of the article, its meaning is clear enough. It does not mean that Christ descended into hell or the place of punishment for lost souls, but into the underworld, the abode of the dead. Rufinus sees in the clause only a repetition of the statement that Christ was buried, and, taken by themselves, the words might imply no more than this (cf. Kattenbusch, II. p. 900 seq.), but in view of their addition to the phrase καὶ ταφέντα instead of their substitution for it in the Aquileian creed, and in view of the traditional belief in the Descent into Hades there can be no doubt that the present article means not simply that Christ died and was laid in the tomb, but that he went down consciously and with a purpose into the underworld, the abode of departed spirits. The belief in such a Descent into Hades is as old as the first century, and it has a large place in the literature of the second century (cf. for instance Acts II. 31; 1 Peter III. 19; IV. 6; Rom. X. 7; Eph. IV. 9; Gospel of Peter; Justin Martyr, *Dial.* 72; Irenæus, IV. 22; IV. 27, 2; Tertullian, *De anima*, 55).

The purpose of the descent was variously understood. Thus it was thought that Christ went down in order to break the doors of Hades and show himself victor over Satan, or to lead thence the patriarchs and prophets and other pious Israelites, or to preach the gospel to the dead, or to complete his work of redemption and free his followers from the control of death, or to share in all respects the lot of men. The idea that Christ went down to suffer the torments of the damned in order to complete thereby his expiatory work arose first in the middle ages.[1]

How the article made its way into the present text of the Apostles' creed we do not know. It occurs very rarely in the symbols known to us, not at all in Africa and only a few times in Western Europe, possibly already in the fifth century (Hahn, §§ 46, 90; see Kattenbusch, II. p. 898), certainly as early as the seventh (Hahn, § 55. On the supposed creed of Venantius Fortunatus given in Hahn, § 38, see Kattenbusch, I. p. 130 seq.)

Upon this article see, in addition to Kattenbusch, Huidekoper, *The Belief of the First Three Centuries concerning Christ's Mission to the Underworld.*

5. The two words *Dei* and *omnipotentis* appear as a part of the article on the session, in Spain as early as the fourth century (Hahn, § 53), and in Gaul as early as the fifth (Hahn, § 61). Later they are common in Spanish texts, but not elsewhere except as a part of our present Apostles' Creed, or of texts influenced by it. *Dei patris* without *omnipotentis* is also common (see Kattenbusch, II. p. 917).

---

[1] For Reformation and modern interpretations of the article see Huidekoper, p. 170 seq.

The addition was evidently due simply to the influence of the first article, and was not intended to change the sense in any way. At the same time it possibly narrows somewhat though unintentionally the scope of *Patris*, which, standing alone in the Old Roman Symbol, suggested at once the Father of the universe, as in the first article, and the Father of Christ. With *Dei omnipotentis* added, of course *Patris* can properly refer only to the Father of the universe.

6. The earliest known appearance of the word catholic in the article on the church is in a text of the fourth century (Hahn, § 45), which is perhaps to be ascribed to Gregory of Elvira in Spain (see Kattenbusch, I. p. 202 seq.). It was common in Gaul after the fourth century (see Hahn, §§ 61, 62, 64 seq.), and in Spain at any rate after the fifth (see Hahn, § 54 seq.). It appears in no North African text and in Italy only at a late date (Hahn, § 37). In the symbol of the church of Jerusalem as reproduced by Cyril (Hahn, § 125; cf. Kattenbusch, I. p. 244) we have εἰς μίαν ἁγίαν καθολικὴν ἐκκλησίαν. In the Nicæno-Constantinopolitan creed and many other eastern symbols we have the fuller phrase καθολικὴν καὶ ἀποστολικὴν ἐκκλησίαν.

It is possible, as maintained by some scholars, that the word was added to the creed in the west under the influence of eastern symbols, or more particularly of the *Catechetics* of Cyril of Jerusalem, but it is more probable that it was added spontaneously, for it was common in the west as well as in the east in the fourth century. It occurs rarely in connection with the church before the third century, but thereafter it was in common use both in east and west, and its insertion in the creed would have been most natural at any time and place, for it was the custom, at any rate from the fourth century on, to speak of the church as the " Holy catholic church." The word catholic means literally universal (καθ' ὅλου), and so the phrase καθολικὴ ἐκκλησία (Latin, *catholica ecclesia*, neither word being translated) means literally " universal church." But the phrase was not intended to mark the distinction between the church at large and the individual church or congregation, for the latter might be as truly καθολική as the former (cf. Ignatius, *Smyrn.* 8 ; *Mart. Polyc.* 16, 19), but rather apparently to indicate the universal purpose or significance of the church. The church was universal, not simply because it was spread everywhere, but because it was for every one, and so belonged to and had a meaning for the whole world.

As time passed and false teaching began to make trouble within the church and to require the exclusion of individuals and bodies of Christians, the phrase καθολικὴ ἐκκλησία came to mean the true Christian church — the one only orthodox church — in distinction from all heretical and schismatic bodies which might call themselves Christian churches, but which in the eyes of Christians in general were not really so. This meaning appears already in the Muratorian fragment, and is common from the third century on. (Cf. Cyril of Jerusalem, *Catechetics*, XVIII. 26.) This true Christian church being a particular visible organized institution, distinguishable from other institutions claiming the name of Christian and more or less similar to it in character, the phrase καθολικὴ ἐκκλησία acquired the force of a mere title or proper name, and so might be used, as it commonly was after the third century, without any thought of the original meaning of the word catholic. When the title was reflected upon and analyzed it was commonly interpreted to mean " existing everywhere " and to refer to the universal spread of the church, which was made much of by polemics over against the local character of the schismatic churches: thus, for instance, by Optatus and Augustine in their controversy with the Donatists. But there is no reason to think that the word "catholic" was added to the creed in order to express a belief in the universality of the church, or in any other of its attributes, but simply as a part of the common and familiar name by which the church was known. Nothing more was meant by *sanctam ecclesiam catholicam* than by *sanctam ecclesiam* alone. To read into the word *catholicam* in the creed therefore a special meaning of its own is not historically justified. It is simply a part of a title, just as to-day "The Catholic Church" is the popular title of the Roman communion.

7. The phrase *sanctorum communionem* appears first as a part of the creed in the text ascribed to Nicetas of Aquileia (Hahn, § 40) which belongs perhaps to Gaul and to the beginning of the fifth century (cf. Kattenbusch, I. p. 108 seq.) The article occurs also a little later in Faustus of Riez (Hahn, § 61) and in the next century in Cæsarius of Arles (Hahn, § 62), and later still in other Gallic texts (Hahn, §§ 66, 67, etc.) It does not appear at all in eastern creeds, or in Italian and North African texts, and in Spain it is found only in the Mozarabic liturgy (Hahn, § 58). It was thus common in Gaul at the time our present Apostles' Creed was framed, but apparently not elsewhere.

In documents of the late fourth and early fifth centuries we find the phrase used in two different senses. Thus in the acts of the Council of Nîmes, held in 394 A. D. (see Hefele, *Conciliengeschichte*, 2d edit., vol. II. p. 61 seq.), the phrase is used to denote participation in sacred things, that is in the sacraments (see Kattenbusch, II. p. 930). In

Nicetas on the other hand (see Caspari, *Anecdota*, I. p. 355 seq.) it signifies communion with the believers of all ages, more particularly with the saints and angels in heaven. The reference here is primarily to the communion to be enjoyed in heaven after death. In the centuries that follow, the phrase is used in both these senses, *sanctorum* being taken sometimes as neuter, and sometimes as masculine (see Kattenbusch, II. p. 931 seq.). In which sense the phrase was understood when it was inserted in the creed we do not know;[1] possibly in both, as Kattenbusch thinks, for the two meanings were closely associated and often appear together in the same writer. Whoever enjoys real participation in the sacraments enjoys also communion with the saints and vice versa.

The interpretation which commonly attaches to the phrase to-day — communion or fellowship of believers with each other — cannot be regarded as correct, for if this were the meaning we should hardly expect *sanctorum* to receive the emphasis which its position before *communio* gives it (cf. Kattenbusch, II. p. 944 note), and moreover this interpretation does not appear until much later, at any rate in that part of the world where

---

[1] Zahn, *Das Apostolische Symbolum*, p. 92, regards the former as the correct interpretation of the article ; belief being expressed by it not that there are sacraments, but that in the sacraments one enjoys participation in the " Heiligtümern der jenseitigen Welt."

the article was first added to the creed. It is commonly supposed that Augustine used the phrase in this sense in his controversy with the Donatists (cf. for instance Zahn, *Das Apostolische Symbolum*, p. 91; Harnack, *Das Apostolische Glaubensbekenntniss*, p. 31; and Swete, *The Apostles' Creed*, p. 83), but Kattenbusch (II. p. 931 seq.) maintains that it is a mistake, and that the phrase occurs in Augustine only in the sense of *communio sacramentorum*. However that may be, Augustine's use of it, as Zahn remarks, cannot be taken to interpret the article in the creed, for the phrase was never a part of the creed in North Africa, and in western Europe, where it first found its way into the symbol, the interpretation in question appears only some centuries later.

And so the interpretation of the word *communio* as if it were a concrete noun and equivalent to *congregatio* (*Gemeinde der Heiligen* as Luther translates the article) is also incorrect. The word is an abstract and is to be taken in the sense of *participation in*, or *fellowship* or *converse with*. The phrase, then, is not to be understood as a definition of *ecclesia*, as if it meant that the holy church catholic is a *communio sanctorum*. This was the interpretation of the Reformers, and has been generally accepted by Protestants, but it is not true to the original meaning of the article in the creed. That the church *has* a *communio sanctorum*, that such *communio* is to be had within or through the church, was often said in the part of the world where the article first got into the creed, but not that the church *is* a *communio sanctorum*.

The purpose of the insertion of the article in the creed we have no means of determining. Harnack, upon the basis of its interpretation in *S. Faustini tractatus de symbolo* (which Caspari publishes in his *Alte und neue Quellen*, p. 250 seq., ascribing its contents but not its form to Faustus of Riez), thinks it was directed against Vigilantius, who opposed saint worship and so was widely believed to be throwing contempt upon the memory of the saints (see Harnack, *Das apostolische Glaubensbekenntniss*, p. 32). But as Kattenbusch rightly says (II. p. 943), the general phrase *sanctorum communionem* does not actually touch the matter of controversy between Vigilantius and the church at large, for Vigilantius believed as truly as anybody in communion with the saints and opposed only the worship of them, or more particularly the worship of their relics. So the article can hardly have been added in opposition to Vigilantius. And in view of the wide diversity of interpretation which we find from the fifth century on, and in view of the uncertainty as to whether *sanctorum* is to be understood of things or persons, we must recognize that it is impossible, at any rate with our present light, to say why it was added.

8. The article *Vitam aeternam* first found its way into the Old Roman Symbol in North Africa, where it occurs already in the time of Cyprian (see Hahn, § 12), and it continued to be a part of the creed there (cf. Hahn, § 47 seq.). It is also found in most eastern symbols, sometimes in a slightly different form (in Hahn, §§ 124 and 126 : ζωὴν αἰώνιον ; in §§ 125, 129, 144 : ζωὴν τοῦ μέλλοντος αἰῶνος), in most West European texts, and in some Italian texts (see Hahn, §§ 35, 37, 40, 41, 54 seq., 58, 61, 62, 64 seq.). It is in fact the most common of all the additions to the Old Roman Symbol. Whether it arose independently in east and west, and independently also in different parts of the west we do not know, but the identity of the phrase in western creeds of all localities suggests a common source at any rate for the Occident. The addition was a natural one to appear at any time and place, for the Old Roman Symbol, when its original purpose had been lost sight of, must seem incomplete, concluding as it did with the resurrection of the flesh. That some reference to the future blessedness of believers should be subjoined was only what might have been expected, and no special polemic interest is needed to explain it.

We learn from Augustine of the existence of doubts as to whether the resurrection was to result in a permanent or only a temporary life, whether, that is, it was to be like the resurrection of Lazarus or the resurrection of Christ, and it is not impossible that it was such doubts that gave the occasion for the addition of the article.[1] But the article had probably found its way into the Old Roman Symbol long before Augustine's day, and it is more likely that it was added spontaneously with the simple desire of giving more adequate expression to the future blessedness of believers. The phrase was the traditional and natural one to express the Christian hope. It is very common in the New Testament, especially in the writings of John, and in the literature of the second and following centuries (see for instance the passages referred to by Harnack, in Hahn, p. 389). The controlling idea attaching to the phrase as employed by John and other New Testament writers is not everlasting life, but life belonging to another and higher order. It is the quality of the life as heavenly, spiritual, divine, not its duration, that they chiefly think of in using the words (see Vincent, *Word Studies in the New Testament*, vol. IV. p. 58 seq.). But the idea of everlasting

---

[1] Cf. Kattenbusch, II. p. 951 seq., who quotes also a passage bearing upon the subject from Chrysostom's fortieth homily on First Corinthians.

duration, which belonged to the Greek word αἰώνιος in philosophical usage, soon attached to it among the Christians (cf., e. g., Justin, *Apol.* I. 8), and has continued ever since, and this meaning was prominent when the article *vitam aeternam* (ζωὴν αἰώνιον) was added to the creed. But the phrase never lost the qualitative value which originally belonged to it. It has always meant, not simply everlasting existence, which may be shared by lost as well as saved, but salvation and eternal blessedness. The apostles' creed, therefore, in its present form closes with an article which sums up in a pregnant gospel phrase the future blessedness of the saved, and is thus in its conclusion far better adapted for permanent use as a Christian creed than the Old Roman Symbol, which ends abruptly with the resurrection of the flesh.

www.ingramcontent.com/pod-product-compliance
Lightning Source LLC
Chambersburg PA
CBHW051923160426
43198CB00012B/2011